EDEXCEL INTERNATIONAL GCSE (9-1)

HISTORY

DICTATORSHIP AND CONFLICT IN THE USSR, 1924–53

Student Book

Simon Taylor

Series Editor: Nigel Kelly

Published by Pearson Education Limited, 80 Strand, London, WC2R 0RL.

www.pearsonglobalschools.com

Copies of official specifications for all Pearson qualifications may be found on the website: https://qualifications.pearson.com

Text © Pearson Education Limited 2017
Edited by Juliet Gardner
Designed by Cobalt id and Pearson Education Limited
Typeset and illustrated by Phoenix Photosetting Ltd, Chatham, Kent
Original illustrations © Pearson Education Limited 2017
Cover design by Pearson Education Limited
Picture research by Sarah Hewitt
Cover photo/illustration © gettyimages.co.uk: Ullstein Bild
Inside front cover Shutterstock.com: Dmitry Lobanov

The rights of Simon Taylor to be identified as author of this work have been asserted by him in accordance with the Copyright, Designs and Patents Act 1988.

First published 2017

20 19 18
10 9 8 7 6 5 4 3 2

British Library Cataloguing in Publication Data
A catalogue record for this book is available from the British Library

ISBN 978 0 435 18546 6

Printed in Slovakia by Neografia

Acknowledgements
The author and publisher would like to thank the following individuals and organisations for permission to reproduce photographs:
(Key: b-bottom; c-centre; l-left; r-right; t-top)

Alamy Stock Photo: akg-images 99, 103, David Cole 11b, Everett Collection Historical 100, GL Archive 48, Granger Historical Picture Archive 10t, Heritage Image Partnership Ltd 9, 39, 49, 57, 60, 64r, Interfoto 11t, 107, Itar-Tass Photo Agency 10c, 15, 58, 61, Joeri De Rocker 38, Pictorial Press Ltd 44, 50, 93, Prisma by Dukas Presseagentur GmbH 64l, Sputnik 52, 53, 70, 77br, 101, World History Archive 8, 10b, 26b;
Getty Images: Culture Club 21, Heritage Images 26t, Hulton Archive 87, James E. Abbe / ullstein bild 2, Margaret Bourke-White 30, 72, Max Penson 43, Popperfoto 106, Sovfoto 75, 77tl, 77bl, Sovfoto / UIG 34, Topical Press Agency 68, ullstein bild 88

All other images © Pearson Education Limited

We are grateful to the following for permission to reproduce copyright material:

Text
Extract on page 73 from *The Russian Revolution (OPUS)*, 2nd Revised ed., Oxford Paperbacks (Fitzpatrick,S.), by permission of Oxford University Press.

Select glossary terms have been taken from *The Longman Dictionary of Contemporary English Online*.

Disclaimer
All maps in this book are drawn to support the key learning points. They are illustrative in style and are not exact representations.

Endorsement Statement
In order to ensure that this resource offers high-quality support for the associated Pearson qualification, it has been through a review process by the awarding body. This process confirms that this resource fully covers the teaching and learning content of the specification or part of a specification at which it is aimed. It also confirms that it demonstrates an appropriate balance between the development of subject skills, knowledge and understanding, in addition to preparation for assessment.

Endorsement does not cover any guidance on assessment activities or processes (e.g. practice questions or advice on how to answer assessment questions), included in the resource nor does it prescribe any particular approach to the teaching or delivery of a related course.

While the publishers have made every attempt to ensure that advice on the qualification and its assessment is accurate, the official specification and associated assessment guidance materials are the only authoritative source of information and should always be referred to for definitive guidance.

Pearson examiners have not contributed to any sections in this resource relevant to examination papers for which they have responsibility.

Examiners will not use endorsed resources as a source of material for any assessment set by Pearson. Endorsement of a resource does not mean that the resource is required to achieve this Pearson qualification, nor does it mean that it is the only suitable material available to support the qualification, and any resource lists produced by the awarding body shall include this and other appropriate resources.

ABOUT THIS BOOK

This book is written for students following the Pearson Edexcel International GCSE (9–1) History specification and covers one unit of the course. This unit is Dictatorship and Conflict in the USSR, 1924–53, one of the Depth Studies. The History course has been structured so that teaching and learning can take place in any order, both in the classroom and in any independent learning. The book contains five chapters which match the five areas of content in the specification:

- The leadership struggle, 1924–29
- Five Year Plans and collectivisation
- Purges, show trials, the cult of Stalin and the revision of history
- Life in the Soviet Union, 1924–41
- The Second World War and after, 1941–53

Each chapter is split into multiple sections to break down content into manageable chunks and to ensure full coverage of the specification.

Each chapter features a mix of learning and activities. Sources are embedded throughout to develop your understanding and exam-style questions help you to put learning into practice. Recap pages at the end of each chapter summarise key information and let you check your understanding. Exam guidance pages help you prepare confidently for the exam.

Learning Objectives Each section starts with a list of what you will learn in it. They are carefully tailored to address key assessment objectives central to the course.

Timeline Visual representation of events to clarify the order in which they happened.

Activity Each chapter includes activities to help check and embed knowledge and understanding.

Source Photos, cartoons and text sources are used to explain events and show you what people from the period said, thought or created, helping you to build your understanding.

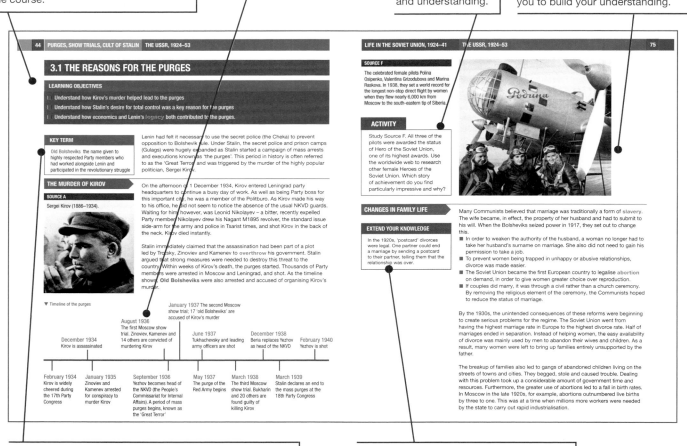

Key term Useful words and phrases are colour coded within the main text and picked out in the margin with concise and simple definitions. These help understanding of key subject terms and support students whose first language is not English.

Extend your knowledge Interesting facts to encourage wider thought and stimulate discussion. They are closely related to key issues and allow you to add depth to your knowledge and answers.

Recap
At the end of each chapter, you will find a page designed to help you consolidate and reflect on the chapter as a whole.

Recall quiz
This quick quiz is ideal for checking your knowledge or for revision.

Exam-style question
Questions tailored to the Pearson Edexcel specification to allow for practice and development of exam writing technique. They also allow for practice responding to the command words used in the exams.

Skills
Relevant exam questions have been assigned the key skills which you will gain from undertaking them, allowing for a strong focus on particular academic qualities. These transferable skills are highly valued in further study and the workplace.

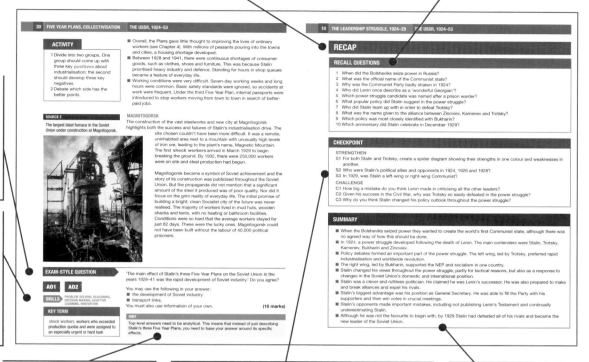

Hint
All exam-style questions are accompanied by a hint to help you get started on an answer.

Checkpoint
Checkpoints help you to check and reflect on your learning. The Strengthen section helps you to consolidate knowledge and understanding, and check that you have grasped the basic ideas and skills. The Challenge questions push you to go beyond just understanding the information, and into evaluation and analysis of what you have studied.

Summary
The main points of each chapter are summarised in a series of bullet points. These are great for embedding core knowledge and handy for revision.

Exam guidance
At the end of each chapter, you will find two pages designed to help you better understand the exam questions and how to answer them. Each exam guidance section focuses on a particular question type that you will find in the exam, allowing you to approach them with confidence.

Student answers
Exemplar student answers are used to show what an answer to the exam question may look like. There are often two levels of answers so you can see what you need to do to write better responses.

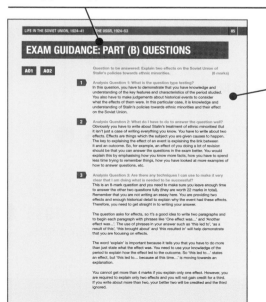

Advice on answering the question
Three key questions about the exam question are answered here in order to explain what the question is testing and what you need to do to succeed in the exam.

Pearson Progression
Sample student answers have been given a Pearson Step from 1 to 12. This tells you how well the response has met the criteria in the Pearson Progression Map.

Commentary
Feedback on the quality of the answer is provided to help you understand their strengths and weaknesses and show how they can be improved.

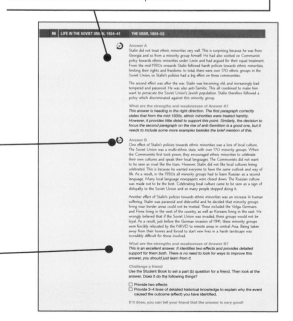

TIMELINE – THE USSR, 1924–53

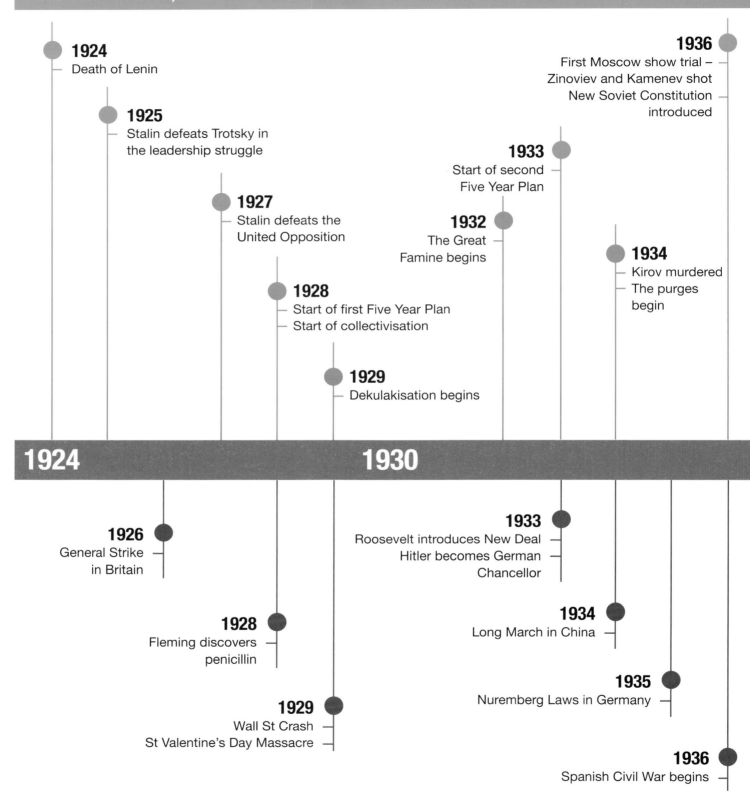

1924
Death of Lenin

1925
Stalin defeats Trotsky in
the leadership struggle

1927
Stalin defeats the
United Opposition

1928
Start of first Five Year Plan
Start of collectivisation

1929
Dekulakisation begins

1932
The Great
Famine begins

1933
Start of second
Five Year Plan

1934
Kirov murdered
The purges
begin

1936
First Moscow show trial –
Zinoviev and Kamenev shot
New Soviet Constitution
introduced

1924

1930

1926
General Strike
in Britain

1928
Fleming discovers
penicillin

1929
Wall St Crash
St Valentine's Day Massacre

1933
Roosevelt introduces New Deal
Hitler becomes German
Chancellor

1934
Long March in China

1935
Nuremberg Laws in Germany

1936
Spanish Civil War begins

TIMELINE – WORLD

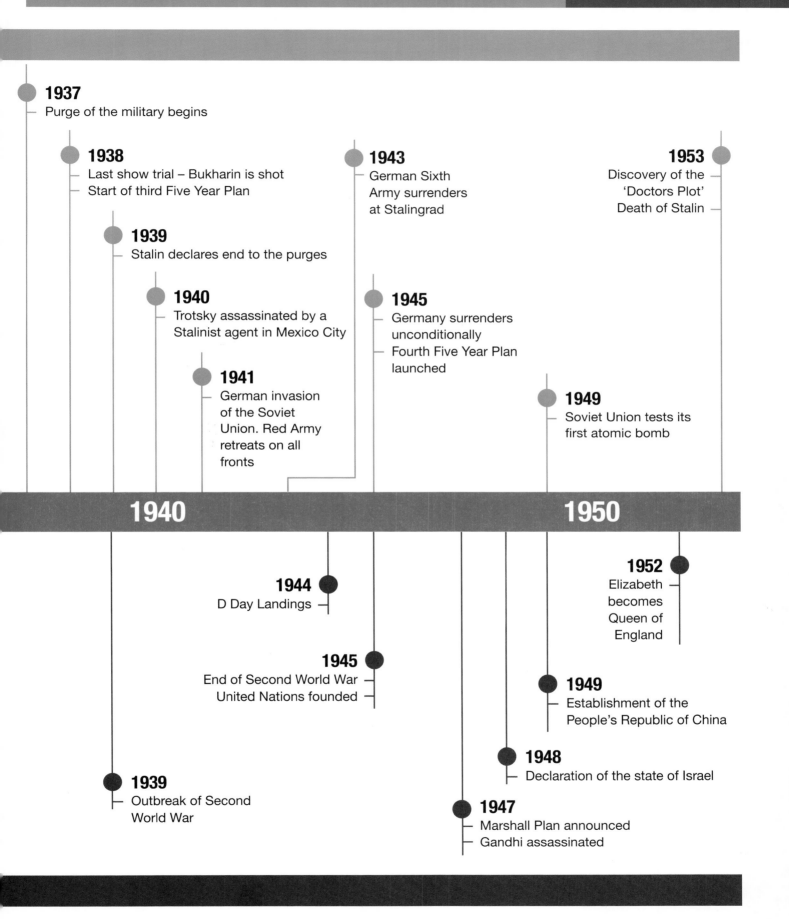

1937
Purge of the military begins

1938
Last show trial – Bukharin is shot
Start of third Five Year Plan

1939
Stalin declares end to the purges

1940
Trotsky assassinated by a
Stalinist agent in Mexico City

1941
German invasion
of the Soviet
Union. Red Army
retreats on all
fronts

1943
German Sixth
Army surrenders
at Stalingrad

1945
Germany surrenders
unconditionally
Fourth Five Year Plan
launched

1949
Soviet Union tests its
first atomic bomb

1953
Discovery of the
'Doctors Plot'
Death of Stalin

1940

1950

1944
D Day Landings

1945
End of Second World War
United Nations founded

1939
Outbreak of Second
World War

1952
Elizabeth
becomes
Queen of
England

1949
Establishment of the
People's Republic of China

1948
Declaration of the state of Israel

1947
Marshall Plan announced
Gandhi assassinated

1. THE LEADERSHIP STRUGGLE, 1924–29

LEARNING OBJECTIVES

☐ Understand who the main contenders were in the fight to become the new leader

☐ Understand the different steps Stalin took to defeat his opponents between 1924–29

☐ Understand why Stalin emerged as leader of the Soviet Union.

In January 1924, Lenin, the leader of the world's first Communist state, died. The Soviet Union went into official mourning. Within 3 days, half a million people had filed past his body to pay their last respects. In the atmosphere of grief, the decision was taken to preserve Lenin's body, while his brain was sliced into 30,000 sections to allow scientists to study his great intellect.

Within the Communist Party itself, a sense of gloom set in. Lenin had offered inspirational leadership, holding the Party together through a revolution and civil war. The ongoing attempt to build a communist system in the Soviet Union was, however, a brave new experiment with no clear rule book. Huge challenges remained, which would now have to be solved without Lenin.

One thing was clear. A new leader was needed for the next stage of the revolution. But who could possibly take on this huge task? By 1929, the answer was clear – the bank robber, prison escapee and tough revolutionary, Joseph Stalin.

1.1 THE SOVIET UNION IN 1924

LEARNING OBJECTIVES

☐ Understand how the Bolsheviks had come to power.

KEY TERM

peasants poor farmers who own or rent a small amount of land

The Soviet Union in 1924 was unique (see Figure 1.1). More than twice the size of the USA, it was the world's largest country. Over 6,000 km separated Vladivostok in the east from the Soviet Union's western border, while it was some 3,000 km from the deserts of the south to the Arctic wastelands in the north. Most of the Soviet Union's 165 million people lived in the rich agricultural lands west of the Ural Mountains. Here too were the largest cities: the capital Moscow, and Leningrad. Only 4 per cent of the Soviet Union's people were industrial workers. Most people (80 per cent of the population) were **peasants**, making their living from the land.

▼ **Figure 1.1** The geographical and political structure of the Soviet Union in 1924

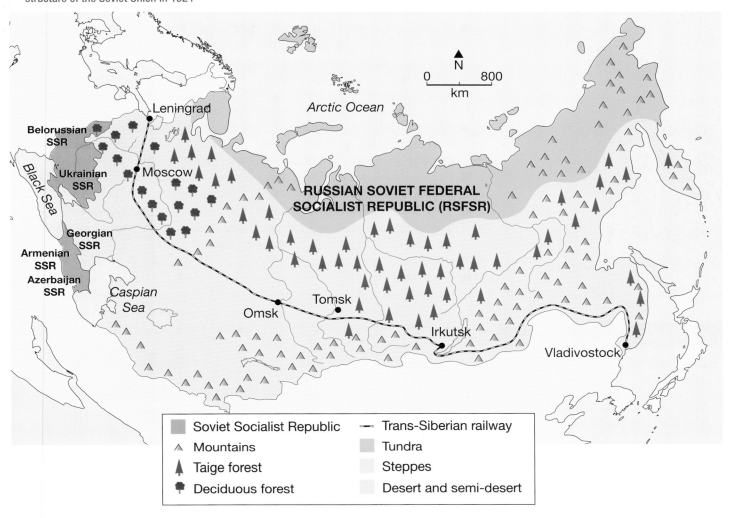

KEY TERM

communist a political system in which the government controls the production of all food and goods, and there is no privately owned property

In 1924, the Soviet Union was unique for another reason. It was aiming to create the world's first **communist** society, in which all people would work together for the common good and be considered equal. The experiment was barely 7 years old and had already brought huge change, chaos and sometimes joy to its people. You do not need to know the details of the period 1917–24 for your exam, but some knowledge of them will help you understand the problems that existed in 1924.

BACKGROUND 1917–24 (NOT IN THE EXAM)

- The Union of Soviet Socialist Republics, also known as the Soviet Union or the USSR, was formally established in 1922. It was made up of five semi-independent **republics** – Georgia, Azerbaijan, Armenia, Ukraine and Belorussia – plus the Russian Soviet Federal Socialist Republic as the largest and most powerful **bloc**.
- In 1914, the First World War broke out. Russia, as the Soviet Union was then called, was ruled by Tsar Nicholas II. He joined France and Britain in fighting Germany and Austria-Hungary.
- In February 1917, a combination of military defeats and severe food shortages led to a popular rebellion against Nicholas II. His decision to give up power ended 300 years of rule by the Romanov royal family.
- A quickly formed '**Provisional** Government' was set up to lead Russia. It promised to bring democracy to the people. However, it continued the war and became increasingly unpopular.
- In October 1917, the Bolsheviks, a small group of dedicated revolutionaries led by Lenin, carried out a daring plan and seized power. Lenin announced that Russia was now a communist state.
- After the October Revolution, Lenin, among other **reforms**, allowed workers to take over the factories, declared women equal to men, ended **private ownership** of land, and made peace with the Germans.
- The Communists, or 'Reds', were only ever supported by a minority of the population, and Russia quickly descended into **civil war**.
- They were opposed by the 'Whites', a badly organised and deeply divided group made up of other left-wing political groups, supporters of the tsar, landlords and businessmen, as well as the armies of 17 foreign nations including Britain, the USA, France and Japan.
- To stand a chance of winning, Lenin reorganised the economy on military lines in a policy known as War Communism. All industry was brought under state control. In order to make sure that the soldiers were fed, rationing was introduced and **grain** was forcibly seized from the peasants. Strict discipline was **imposed** on factory workers, including fines for being late. In addition, private trade was banned and money was no longer used.
- During the war, the Communists used terror to maintain control. For example, in the city of Oryol, some 3,500 km south of Moscow, opponents were allowed to freeze to death and then put on display as ice statues.
- By 1921 the Communists had won, but at a huge cost. The economy was in ruins. Industrial and agricultural production was below pre-First World War levels. There was a major **famine** in 1921, resulting in millions of deaths.

KEY TERMS

grain the seeds of crops such as corn, wheat or rice

famine where a large number of people have little or no food for a long time

EXTEND YOUR KNOWLEDGE

EXTEND YOUR KNOWLEDGE

The Bolsheviks based their ideas of communism on the writings of Karl Marx. A 19th-century German philosopher, Marx believed that all societies pass through a series of stages before reaching communism (see Figure 1.2), which would be based upon the following principle: 'From each according to his ability, to each according to his needs.' This means each person takes what they need and contributes what they can.

▶ **Figure 1.2** The stages in Marx's theory of history

KEY TERM

New Economic Policy a policy that reversed many radical measures introduced during the Civil War. People could own their own businesses and make money

By 1924 some measure of stability had returned to the Soviet Union. Although Lenin had wanted to bring about **radical** change in the country, he was realistic: the First World War, followed by 3 years of civil war, had pushed the Russian people to breaking point. So the government had begun to adopt more **moderate** policies. War Communism was replaced by the **New Economic Policy** (see Chapter 2, page 22). Lenin believed that once the country had recovered, the pace of change could be increased.

But time was not on Lenin's side. In poor health after being wounded in an **assassination** attempt, he suffered a series of strokes in 1922 and 1923 that left him **paralysed** and unable to speak. The hero of the October Revolution died in January 1924.

Stage 1: Primitive communism
In the Stone Age, all people were equal and shared the work according to their talents. They had an equal share of everything that was produced.

Stage 2: Feudalism
In the Middle Ages, all the land belonged to the king, who shared it with his lords. The majority of the people were peasants, who were exploited for their labour and owned by their lords.

Stage 3: Capitalism
The growth of trade and industry in the 18th and 19th centuries allowed a rich class of business owners – or capitalists, as Marx called them – to develop. Capitalists drew huge profits from the labour of their workers, called the proletariat. They paid their workers only a small fraction of the money made from their labour.

Stage 4: Communism
The exploitation of the workers under capitalism would lead them to rise up against the capitalists in a revolution. After the revolution, a state of equality would be achieved in which there would be no classes and business, and all property would be owned by the whole of society.

EXAM-STYLE QUESTION

A01   **A02**

Explain **two** effects on the Soviet Union of Lenin's death in 1924.   **(8 marks)**

HINT

Remember, if you only deal with one consequence, the maximum you can get is 4 marks.

1.2 THE RIVALS FOR LEADERSHIP

LENIN'S TESTAMENT

SOURCE A

Excerpts from Lenin's testament, written in December 1922.

Comrade Stalin has unlimited authority concentrated in his hands, and I am not sure whether he will always be capable of using that authority with sufficient caution... Stalin is too rude.... That is why I suggest the comrades think about a way of removing Stalin from that post and appointing another man... more tolerant, more loyal, more polite, and more considerate to the comrades... Comrade Trotsky, on the other hand, is personally perhaps the most capable man in the present Central Committee, but he has displayed excessive self-assurance and shown excessive preoccupation with the purely administrative side of the work.

KEY TERMS

worldwide revolution the idea that the main job of the Party should be to spread revolution to more advanced countries

socialism in one country the idea that Russia could successfully create a communist state without outside help. Its success would then encourage workers around the world to rise up

Politburo the leading decision-making body in the Communist Party

In his last few months, Lenin knew that the success of the Communist experiment was far from guaranteed. It had to overcome continuing threats from abroad, as well as the huge task of rebuilding the war-devastated country. Furthermore, major decisions were needed on how best to turn the Soviet Union from an old-fashioned agricultural society into a modern, **industrialised** nation. In particular, the Communist Party needed to decide on the following.

■ Should the Party focus on spreading **worldwide revolution**, or concentrate on building **socialism in one country**?

■ Should the Party follow a policy of rapid industrialisation and quickly develop Russia's industrial base, or would it be better to keep the New Economic Policy (NEP) and build factories at a much slower pace?

The quality of leadership in the Party was more crucial than ever before. However, when Lenin considered who should succeed him, he could find no easy answer.

In December 1922, after his second stroke, Lenin turned his thoughts into a 'Testament', to be read after his death. As Source A shows, Lenin recognised that his successor was likely to be either Trotsky or Stalin. In his view, Trotsky was brilliant but too arrogant.

However, the toughest criticism was reserved for Stalin. Lenin had become increasingly worried at Stalin's growing power. As General Secretary of the Communist Party, Stalin had control over appointments and was abusing this position by filling the Party with his own supporters. But the most revealing episode for Lenin took place closer to home. When Lenin's wife, Krupskaya, refused to let Stalin see him, Stalin hit back with a string of crude and abusive insults. Therefore the message of the Testament was clear: Stalin had to go.

Lenin also mentioned but rejected the other leading members of the **Politburo**. Bukharin was popular but did not fully understand Marxism. Zinoviev and Kamenev had destroyed their chances by failing to support the October Revolution.

Why did Lenin criticise all his potential successors? Perhaps he thought that individually, none of them was up to the job of replacing him as leader and, instead, he wanted them to work together. At the end of his life, though, Lenin feared Stalin.

Following Lenin's death, his Testament was temporarily put to one side. Instead Stalin, Trotsky, Kamenev, Bukharin and Zinoviev announced that they would share power. But this show of unity was just an illusion. In reality, each of them wanted either to dominate the Party or else to stop their rivals from gaining the top job. Rather than purposeful collective leadership, the period 1924–29 turned into a long and troubled power struggle.

ACTIVITY

It is 1924, and you are a senior member of the Russian Communist Party. Following on from Lenin's death, you have been given the task of finding Russia's next leader.

1 Working in small groups, study the list below and decide on the five most important qualities a new leader should have. Which qualities do you think are not as important? Make sure you have reasons for your choices.
   - An excellent public speaker
   - A hero of the Civil War
   - Able to be **ruthless**
   - A good organiser
   - Popular among ordinary Party members
   - Efficient at doing paperwork and routine tasks
   - A loyal member of the Party
   - A long-term friend of Lenin
   - An important player in the October 1917 revolution
   - Someone with moderate views
   - Excellent knowledge of Marxist theory
   - Able to win arguments in debates
   - Good at seeking compromise
   - Having a clear vision for how to build communism in Russia
   - Able to dominate meetings and discussions
   - Having a history of disagreeing with Lenin.

2 You now need to produce a job advert. This will include a full job description, the benefits and challenges of the role, as well as a list of the essential and desirable qualities that any candidate will need. Remember to spend time on excellent presentation. You want as many people to read the advert as possible.

THE LEADERSHIP CONTENDERS

STALIN

- Stalin was born in 1879 in the mountainous and lawless kingdom of Georgia in the south of the Russian **Empire**.
- Stalin had a tough childhood and grew up in poverty. His father was a shoemaker, an alcoholic and often violent. As a boy, Stalin caught smallpox, leaving his face scarred, while an accident permanently damaged his left arm.
- Stalin was sent to church school to train as a priest, but instead developed a deep hatred for the Tsarist system and became a Communist **revolutionary**.
- He joined the Bolshevik Party in 1903 and became a tough activist, organising bank robberies to raise Party funds. He was arrested frequently and was twice **exiled** to Siberia, but escaped each time.
- Stalin did not play a glorious role in the October Revolution and the Civil War, but worked hard on many committees. In 1918 he was sent to

organise the defence of Tsaritsyn (later renamed Stalingrad), but he refused to carry out Trotsky's orders, which led to his recall to Moscow. This would contribute to Stalin's deep hatred of Trotsky.

■ Until he fell out with Stalin in 1923, Lenin admired him for his humble origins, hard work and organisational abilities. After the revolution, Lenin appointed Stalin as Commissar for Nationalities, responsible for overseeing the affairs of all the non-Russians within the Soviet Union.

■ Stalin was also made General Secretary. This was considered a boring job as it involved running the administration of the Communist Party, but it made Stalin very powerful in the Party.

■ Stalin was regarded by his colleagues as a political moderate, who generally kept a low profile in meetings. His main contribution to the political debate was the theory of socialism in one country. This stated that the Soviet Union could successfully build a communist state without the need for outside help.

EXAM-STYLE QUESTION

A04

SKILLS ANALYSIS, INTERPRETATION, CREATIVITY

Study Extract A below. What impression does the author give about Stalin as a politician? You must use Extract A to explain your answer. **(6 marks)**

HINT

To do well in this question, you need to identify one overall impression and provide evidence from the extract to explain this, including, for example, the author's use of language and selection of evidence.

EXTRACT A

From the biography entitled *Stalin*, published in 1966.

In the Politburo, when matters of high policy were under debate, Stalin never seemed to impose his views on his colleagues. He carefully followed the course of debate to see what way the wind was blowing and then voted with the majority, unless he had worked out what most people would think beforehand. He was therefore always on the side of the majority. To people in the Party audiences he appeared as a man without personal grudge... who criticised others only for the sake of the cause.

SOURCE B

Photographs of Stalin taken by the Tsarist secret police in 1911.

EXTEND YOUR KNOWLEDGE

In order to protect their identities and their families, revolutionaries often adopted different names. Vladimir Ilyich Ulyanov chose the name Lenin to remind him of his time in Siberian exile, close to the Lena river. Lev Bronstein called himself Leon Trotsky after one of his prison guards, whose passport he used to escape. The name Stalin, born Joseph Dzhugashvili, means 'man of steel'.

TROTSKY

- Born in 1879 into a wealthy Jewish farming family in the Ukraine, Trotsky was a talented school and university student. He was arrested in 1898 for revolutionary activities, and after 2 years in prison was sentenced to 4 years' exile in Siberia. In 1902, hidden in a hay wagon, he escaped.

- In 1905, Trotsky made his revolutionary name by taking a leading role in a large-scale but unsuccessful uprising against the tsar. After escaping from Russia, he spent the next 12 years abroad, including periods in Britain, Austria-Hungary, France, Switzerland, Spain and the USA.

- Until 1917, Trotsky had a difficult relationship with Lenin. He refused to join the Bolsheviks because he opposed Lenin's ideas of a small, secretive but highly organised political party.

- Nevertheless, in 1917 Trotsky returned to Russia, and became a Bolshevik and also Lenin's right-hand man. Together they planned and led the October Revolution.

- In 1918, Trotsky became the Commissar for War. He created the Red Army and led the Bolsheviks to victory in the Civil War. He directed operations from a specially armoured train, complete with a Rolls-Royce command car, equipped with two machine guns.

- Trotsky was highly regarded in the Party for his charisma and inspirational speech making, but many disliked him personally because of his extreme arrogance.

- Trotsky wanted to promote worldwide revolution since he believed that without this, the Soviet Union's own efforts to build communism would fail. He also wanted to follow a policy of rapid industrialisation, despite the strain that this would place on society.

- For 3 years from 1923, Trotsky suffered attacks of an unknown fever, which required long periods of recovery.

SOURCE C

Leon Trotsky during the Civil War, with his armed body guards.

THE OTHER LEADERSHIP CONTENDERS

At the start of the power struggle, three other members of the Politburo, besides Stalin and Trotsky, wanted to become the Soviet Union's new leader (see Figure 1.3). However, they were not regarded as major contenders.

▼ Figure 1.3 The other leadership contenders

☆ SHORTLIST OF PARTY CONTENDERS, 1924 ☆

Leader of the Party

Kamenev

Background
- Working-class upbringing
- Joined the Bolsheviks when the party was formed in 1903
- Became Lenin's close friend when they were in exile abroad
- Spent time in Siberian exile with Stalin
- Currently Head of the Moscow Communist Party and acting head of the Soviet government
- Supports rapid industrialisation and the ending of the NEP

Not suitable for shortlisting
- ✗ Opposed Lenin's plans for the October Revolution
- ✗ Played little part in the Civil War
- ✗ Too cautious – prefers compromise to confrontation

Bukharin

Background
- Born into a family of teachers
- Endured arrest, imprisonment and exile as a Bolshevik in Tsarist times
- Helped the Bolsheviks seize power in Moscow during the October Revolution
- Popular young politician, described by Lenin as the Party's 'golden boy'
- Brilliant thinker and political writer, who also enjoys painting and poetry
- Currently Editor of *Pravda*, the Party's most important political newspaper
- Supports the NEP and opposes rapid industrialisation

Not suitable for shortlisting
- ✗ Too inexperienced for the hard task of ruling the Soviet Union
- ✗ Disagreed with Lenin about the meaning of Marxism
- ✗ His strong support for the NEP is unpopular with many in the Party

Zinoviev

Background
- Born the son of a prosperous farmer
- Joined the Bolsheviks in 1903
- Fear of arrest led him to flee Russia, where he joined Lenin in exile
- Viewed by Lenin as a close friend
- Currently Head of the Comintern and the Communist Party in Leningrad
- In favour of rapid industrialisation, opposes the NEP

Not suitable for shortlisting
- ✗ Opposed seizing power in the October Revolution
- ✗ Gained a reputation in the Civil War for staying in luxurious hotels, far from the fighting
- ✗ Not popular in the Party – widely seen as vain and not very talented

1.3 STRENGTHS AND WEAKNESSES OF STALIN AND TROTSKY

LEARNING OBJECTIVES

☐ Understand Stalin's advantages in the struggle for the leadership

☐ Understand the strengths and weaknesses of Stalin in the struggle for the leadership

☐ Understand the strengths and weaknesses of Trotsky in the struggle for the leadership.

Despite the young energy of Bukharin, or Zinoviev's and Kamenev's long relationships with Lenin, the leadership contest developed into a struggle between two bitter rivals: Stalin and Trotsky. Figure 1.4 shows how the two men compared at the start of the race for the top job.

▼ **Figure 1.4** Stalin and Trotsky consider their own strengths and weaknesses

Stalin's advantages
- Ordinary Party members like me because they see me as a straight-talking Georgian peasant.
- I have a long history as a Bolshevik. In the name of my Party, I have robbed banks, suffered imprisonment and exile to Siberia.
- Lenin liked and respected me, because of my loyalty and my ability to get things done. He even called me his 'wonderful Georgian'.
- People are tired of war and revolution, so they like my policy of 'socialism in one country'.
- As a member of the Politburo, I'm one of Russia's leading politicians.
- Taking on boring but important jobs has made me powerful in the Party.
- As General Secretary, I can promote my own supporters into key positions.
- Many thousands of workers are joining the Party under a scheme called the 'Lenin Enrolment'. They know that if they want to get on in the Party, they need to support me.
- As General Secretary, I can study over 26,000 personal files on Party members and gather lots of useful information on my opponents.
- My childhood was difficult, but it's made me tough. I'm ready for a political fight and I can be ruthless if I need to.

Stalin's weaknesses
- Lenin's Political Testament calls for my removal, and coming from the Party's highest authority, this could ruin my leadership hopes.
- While I am good at office work, I am a bit of a dull personality. I rarely take the lead in meetings and I'm not a great public speaker or thinker. Trotsky calls me a 'grey blur', 'comrade card-index' or 'arch-mediocrity', and others agree.
- Although I work hard, I didn't take a leading role in the October Revolution or Civil War.

Trotsky's strengths
- Although not an 'Old Bolshevik', I have a long revolutionary history and even took part in the failed 1905 uprising against the tsar.
- I was Lenin's right-hand man from 1917 until his death.
- Working with Lenin, I planned the October Revolution which brought Communist rule to Russia.
- I'm a war hero. I created the Red Army and helped win the Civil War.
- I'm popular among the younger, more radical members of the Party.
- My track record shows I'm a brilliant organiser and can get things done.
- I am very intelligent and after Lenin, I am the Party's greatest thinker.
- I am seen as an inspirational public speaker and can often win people round to my view.
- I am powerful because I have important positions in the Party and government. I'm a member of the Politburo and in charge of the Red Army.

Trotsky's weaknesses
- I only became a Bolshevik in the summer of 1917, so many doubt my commitment to the Party.
- Although I'm brilliant, many people think I'm arrogant. My sarcasm offends many Party members.
- Unfortunately some Party members are anti-Semitic and dislike me because I'm Jewish.
- At important moments when I need to be most active, I often fall ill with a fever and it leaves me exhausted for long periods.
- As I've lived outside Russia for so long, many Party members find me too 'Western'.
- I do not like political tactics. I rarely attend Party meetings and I haven't tried to build up a large body of supporters in the Party.
- I don't think Stalin is a serious threat to me.
- Many people oppose my idea of worldwide revolution because they fear it will lead to new wars and violence. They also think my plan for rapid industrialisation will involve too much suffering for ordinary people.
- Because I'm in charge of the Red Army, some Party members see me as a danger to the revolution and think I will use force to get my own way.

ACTIVITY

1 You have now read about the two main contenders for the leadership of the Communist Party, Stalin and Trotsky. Complete your own version of the following table to summarise their strengths and weaknesses. Rate them in order of how suitable they are.

	▽ REVOLUTIONARY RECORD	▽ RELATIONSHIP WITH LENIN	▽ PARTY APPEAL	▽ POSITIONS OF RESPONSIBILITY	▽ POLICY OUTLOOK	▽ OVERALL RATING
Stalin						
Trotsky						

2 Design a campaign poster for your preferred candidate, explaining why they should become the new leader of Russia. You should comment on the things that mattered to Party members at the time, including each candidate's revolutionary record, relationship with Lenin, policy outlook and position within the Party.

3 Most people at the time thought Trotsky would easily win the power struggle. Indeed, a secret British intelligence report described him as 'the most powerful figure in Russian Bolshevism'. Do you think they were right to say this?

1.4 STALIN'S STEPS TO POWER, 1924–29

LEARNING OBJECTIVES

- Understand the steps taken by Stalin to ensure all of his rivals were defeated by 1929
- Understand how Stalin defeated his rivals
- Understand the reason why Stalin was able to win unchallenged power in the Soviet Union.

All members of the Communist Party had the same overall vision. They wanted to build a communist society. However, there was strongly divided opinion on how best to do this, which led to the creation of hostile wings within the Party.

- The left wing were radicals who wanted to build communism as rapidly as possible. This would require ending the NEP, launching rapid industrialisation and spreading worldwide revolution. Its main figures were Trotsky, Zinoviev and Kamenev.
- The right wing, led by Bukharin, supported the NEP and the slow industrialisation of Russia. They also supported Stalin's idea of socialism in one country. They accepted that it would be a long time before Russia became a communist society, but argued that daily life would be easier for ordinary people.
- For most of the 1920s, Stalin avoided taking extreme positions and so was seen to be in the centre of the Party. He wanted to keep the NEP, but for only as long as it worked. He wanted Russia to industrialise at a faster rate than the right wing did, but not at the breakneck speed demanded by the left wing.

These policy debates formed the background to the power struggle, which, as Figure 1.5 shows, was carried out over three stages.

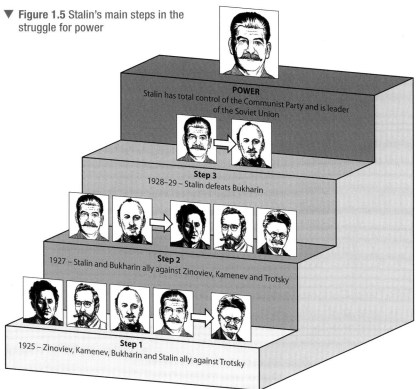

▼ **Figure 1.5** Stalin's main steps in the struggle for power

POWER
Stalin has total control of the Communist Party and is leader of the Soviet Union

Step 3
1928–29 – Stalin defeats Bukharin

Step 2
1927 – Stalin and Bukharin ally against Zinoviev, Kamenev and Trotsky

Step 1
1925 – Zinoviev, Kamenev, Bukharin and Stalin ally against Trotsky

Before Stalin could start defeating his rivals, Lenin had to be buried and the problem of his Testament dealt with. Both tasks went well for Stalin. He saw that it would be good for him to take the lead role in Lenin's funeral, delivering the main speech. As Source D shows, Stalin used the funeral to present himself as Lenin's loyal follower – he simply wanted to continue Lenin's good work. Given Lenin's huge popularity in the Party, this was a clever move. In contrast, Trotsky didn't even attend. This may have been due to illness or, as Trotsky later claimed, because he was tricked by Stalin, who gave him the wrong funeral date. Whatever the reason, Trotsky appeared rude and arrogant and lost support as a result.

In May 1924, Lenin's wife gave his Testament to the **Central Committee**. With its strong criticism of Stalin, it had the potential to ruin his prospects. When its contents were read out, Stalin sat in silence. He was, however, saved as a result of a major error by his fellow contenders. Zinoviev and Kamenev successfully argued that it should not be released to the wider Party. They did this because:

■ the Testament also contained embarrassing remarks about them, which they didn't want to be made public
■ they did not see Stalin as a threat in the power struggle
■ they thought the Testament might help Trotsky, as it contained many positive comments about him.

Trotsky was also at the meeting and went along with the decision, although it is not clear why. Stalin's leadership hopes had survived. With the foundation prepared, the task of dividing and destroying his four rivals could begin.

KEY TERM

Central Committee a section within the Party of around 30–40 members who discussed and voted on key issues

EXTEND YOUR KNOWLEDGE

One of Stalin's great passions was reading, both for enjoyment and as a way to improve himself. To achieve this aim, he could be ruthless. For example, while in exile, when a fellow prisoner died, Stalin took all of his books and refused to share them with anyone else. Stalin's own personal library eventually totalled 20,000 volumes. This passion also had a darker motive. 'If you want to know the people around you,' Stalin said, 'find out what they read.'

SOURCE D

An excerpt from Stalin's funeral speech to Lenin:

In leaving us, Comrade Lenin ordered us to keep the unity of our Party as the apple of our eye. We swear to thee, Comrade Lenin, to honour thy command.

In leaving us, Comrade Lenin ordered us to strengthen with all our might the union of workers and peasants. We swear to thee, Comrade Lenin, to honour thy command.

STEP 1. THE DEFEAT OF TROTSKY

Trotsky was seen as the man most likely to win the power struggle. As a result, the other contenders were prepared to work together to prevent this from happening. After Lenin's death, Stalin, Kamenev and Zinoviev formed an anti-Trotsky **alliance**, broadly supporting the NEP. Working together, they were able to dominate the Party. It did not matter that Kamenev and Zinoviev actually agreed with Trotsky on many things, including the need for rapid industrialisation. They felt it was more important to keep him out of power.

For Stalin, this alliance was an effective tactic. He lacked the authority in the Party to take on Trotsky alone. He also benefited from the way that Zinoviev and Kamenev steadily destroyed Trotsky's reputation as a great Communist and loyal follower of Lenin.

- In speeches and articles, they highlighted all the disagreements that Trotsky had with Lenin, before he became a Bolshevik in 1917.
- They claimed that Trotsky exaggerated his role in the October Revolution.

Stalin rarely contributed to these arguments. He had no need to. Zinoviev and Kamenev were destroying his chief rival for him.

The decisive showdown came at the 1924 Thirteenth **Party Congress**. Trotsky made speeches calling for rapid industrialisation and also greater democracy in the Party. But Stalin had taken care to ensure that Congress was packed full of his supporters. When the votes were counted, Trotsky's proposals had all been rejected.

The Thirteenth Party Congress was a major defeat for Trotsky. In 1925, he lost his position as head of the Red Army and then left active politics. But Trotsky was also partly to blame for his loss of influence. He refused to take part in what he saw as trivial politics by making alliances and growing his own body of supporters in Congress. The decision to attack the lack of democracy in the Party was also a bad tactic. The Party was Lenin's creation, so it seemed as though Trotsky was indirectly criticising their former leader.

KEY TERM

Party Congress made up of representatives from across the Soviet Union, it set the main policies of the Communist Party

EXTEND YOUR KNOWLEDGE

Despite the many bitter arguments of 1924–25, it was noticed that, at meetings of the Central Committee, Stalin would shake hands with Trotsky, but Zinoviev would not. Stalin was skilful at appearing moderate. Also, unlike many others, he kept his thoughts to himself. A fellow Communist once remarked that Stalin spoke little, in a country where everybody else said too much.

STEP 2. THE DEFEAT OF THE UNITED OPPOSITION

Following Trotsky's defeat, the anti-Trotsky alliance split apart. It had achieved its goal. With one rival weakened, Stalin moved onto the next step by forming an alliance with Bukharin and the right wing of the Party. Once again, this was a sensible move.

The two men shared similar views. Bukharin supported Stalin's policy of socialism in one country, and both saw the need to continue with the NEP. Importantly, these policies were supported by the majority of the Party at the time. Socialism in one country was seen as **patriotic**, as it meant that the Soviet Union could build communism without outside help. The NEP, although widely seen as a retreat from communism, was at least giving the country time to recover.

KEY TERM

patriotic having or expressing a great love of your country

The alliance had other advantages. Bukharin had the support of the right wing of the Party and he controlled the media. By working with Stalin, the two men were able to dominate the Party.

Kamenev and Zinoviev had not given up on their own leadership hopes, and in 1926 they put aside their earlier differences with Trotsky, and with him formed the United Opposition. They called for rapid industrialisation, world revolution and the ending of the NEP. The United Opposition hoped to present their case at the 1927 Fifteenth Party Congress. However, they had made a mistake, which in turn had major effects.

- They lost respect. It looked bizarre that Kamenev and Zinoviev were now allies with their former enemy, Trotsky.
- Congress was packed full of Stalin's supporters, who greeted Kamenev and Zinoviev in particular with yells and insults.

- As the United Opposition were now an organised group arguing against approved Party policy, Stalin accused them of '**factionalism**' – something outlawed by Lenin in 1921. Congress supported Stalin.
- As a result of this, Congress **expelled** all three from the Party.

Zinoviev and Kamenev were later allowed back in after admitting they had been wrong, but their authority was destroyed. Trotsky refused to back down. Therefore, in 1929, he was expelled from the Soviet Union, never to return.

KEY TERM

factionalism creating an organised opposition group (faction) inside the Communist Party against its leadership and/or policies

SOURCE E

From left to right, Stalin, Rykov (a member of the Politburo, heavy drinker and supporter of the NEP), Zinoviev and Bukharin, pictured in January 1927 in a surprisingly relaxed setting.

ACTIVITY

Study Source E.
1 What was the political outlook of Stalin, Zinoviev and Bukharin when the photograph was taken?
2 This photo was released to the Soviet press. Why do you think the people in it agreed to this photograph being taken?

STEP 3. THE DEFEAT OF BUKHARIN

Three of the five contenders for power had been removed. Stalin now just needed to deal with Bukharin, who seemed to be in a strong position as he controlled the media and was a favourite of many members of the Party.

Nevertheless, Stalin's control over the Party, combined with his willingness to use clever tactics, ensured Bukharin's rapid defeat. In 1928, Stalin performed a dramatic U-turn and adopted the policies of the left wing. He rejected the NEP in favour of rapid industrialisation. Stalin showed that he meant business by travelling to Siberia, where he gave orders for grain to be violently seized from the peasants. The NEP, which had always stressed co-operation with the peasants, was now at an end.

ACTIVITY

Your challenge is to show the various stages of the power struggle in a series of pictures. Be as creative as possible and try to keep the words to a minimum. Possible ideas could include a boxing match with different rounds, a Formula 1 car race or a witty cartoon.

This U-turn in policy made sense for two reasons.
- The general mood in the Party was starting to shift against the NEP as its failures became apparent. Not enough grain was reaching the cities. Meanwhile, wild rumours spread of a planned invasion from the West, suggesting the need to industrialise so that the Soviet Union could protect itself.
- Adopting the policies of the left gave Stalin a strong identity in the Party, something which he had been lacking as the 'grey blur'.

When Bukharin attempted to defend the NEP in Party meetings, he was simply outvoted. There was nothing that he could do, and Stalin ensured that Bukharin lost his most important posts. In a long and dishonest power struggle, Stalin was the last man standing.

THE REASONS BEHIND STALIN'S VICTORY IN THE LEADERSHIP STRUGGLE

In December 1929, Stalin celebrated his 50th birthday. The poor child from Georgia had come a long way. He was now the unchallenged leader of the Soviet Union.

Four main reasons help explain this achievement, as shown in Figure 1.6.

THE IMPORTANCE OF POLICIES

Party policy mattered to members of the Communist Party. After all, many had led dangerous uncomfortable lives fighting for the revolution and they wanted to make sure their next leader would deliver the future they had long dreamed of. Part of Stalin's success lay in his ability to suggest the right policies at the right time. Two examples illustrate this.

■ Stalin's policy of socialism in one country won him wide support. It was a positive, patriotic message, which contrasted well with Trotsky's call for worldwide revolution. This sounded impractical, especially as it became clear that the advanced nations of the West were not going to rise up.

■ Stalin's decision to argue for rapid industrialisation in 1928 was widely supported. By this stage, the NEP was unpopular and the Party's desire for extreme solutions had been reawakened by food shortages in the cities and by fears of foreign invasion.

▶ **Figure 1.6** The reasons for Stalin's victory in the struggle for power

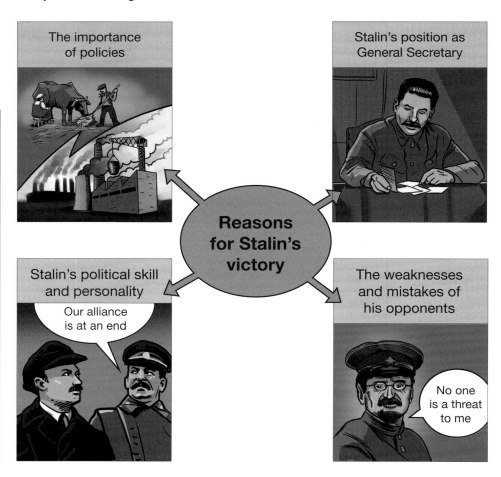

ACTIVITY

In small groups, read the following statements and discuss how far you agree with each one. Remember to record your reasons.

1 Stalin was the weakest of all the contenders for power.
2 Lenin wanted Trotsky to succeed him.
3 Kamenev and Zinoviev deserve praise for their role in the power struggle.
4 Stalin's greatest advantage was his position as General Secretary.
5 The Communist Party members were not interested in policy.
6 Lenin helped Stalin's rise to power.

STALIN'S POSITION AS GENERAL SECRETARY

Stalin, however, did not win on the strength of his policy arguments alone. He benefited greatly from his position as General Secretary. By controlling appointments and promotions within the Party, he was able to fill it steadily with his own supporters. When it came to voting against Trotsky's policy of rapid industrialisation, expelling the United Opposition or dismissing Bukharin's NEP arguments, for example, Stalin knew that he could always count on a majority.

STALIN'S POLITICAL SKILL AND PERSONALITY

Stalin only became General Secretary because no one else wanted the position. It was regarded as a boring post. In fact, his rivals enjoyed joking about the attention that Stalin paid to paperwork – he was known as 'comrade card index'. Stalin's ability to turn this position into a powerful weapon highlights another reason behind his victory: he was skilled at political plotting. This was demonstrated by the clever way he took advantage of Lenin's funeral, his willingness to make and break alliances, as well as his use of Lenin's ban on factions to silence his opponents.

It would be wrong to see Stalin as just a ruthless politician. Many people were prepared to support him because they liked his personality. They regarded Stalin as humble, ordinary and straightforward. As the **Lenin Enrolment** was bringing in thousands of politically basic workers, being seen as a 'man of the people', rather than a high-flying intellectual, was a positive advantage.

KEY TERM

Lenin Enrolment between 1923 and 1925 the Party recruited over 500,000 new members from the working class. They were mainly poorly educated and not very knowledgeable about communist theory. As General Secretary, Stalin supervised the enrolment

THE WEAKNESSES AND MISTAKES OF HIS OPPONENTS

Stalin's rise to power was certainly made easier by his rivals. On paper he was dull and uninspiring, and should not have been able to win against shining stars like Trotsky or Bukharin. However, reality proved very different.
- Trotsky, for all his achievements, was unpopular. He saw no need to control his arrogance, or build friendships and alliances in the wider Party. He made huge errors of judgement in failing to attend Lenin's funeral, or argue for the publication of his Testament.
- Zinoviev and Kamenev proved to be poor politicians who failed to realise that Stalin was a serious rival. As a result, they successfully argued for Lenin's Testament to be kept secret. They also miscalculated by entering into an alliance with Stalin against Trotsky.
- Bukharin simply lacked the political skills needed to fight Stalin.

As we shall see in Chapter 3, Stalin's rivals would pay a high price for their failure.

EXAM-STYLE QUESTION

A01   **A02**

SKILLS PROBLEM SOLVING, REASONING, DECISION MAKING, ADAPTIVE LEARNING, INNOVATION

'The main reason that Stalin won the leadership struggle of 1924–29 was his policy of socialism in one country.' How far do you agree? Explain your answer.

You may use the following in your answer:
- Stalin's policy of socialism in one country
- Stalin's position as General Secretary.

You **must** also use information of your own.   **(16 marks)**

HINT

To do well in this question, make sure you identify at least one additional factor beyond the stimulus points. Make sure that you have accurate and relevant historical knowledge to expand on each of your key points.

RECAP

RECALL QUESTIONS

1 When did the Bolsheviks seize power in Russia?
2 What was the official name of the Communist state?
3 Why was the Communist Party badly shaken in 1924?
4 Who did Lenin once describe as a 'wonderful Georgian'?
5 Which power struggle candidate was named after a prison warder?
6 What popular policy did Stalin suggest in the power struggle?
7 Who did Stalin team up with in order to defeat Trotsky?
8 What was the name given to the alliance between Zinoviev, Kamenev and Trotsky?
9 Which policy was most closely identified with Bukharin?
10 Which anniversary did Stalin celebrate in December 1929?

CHECKPOINT

STRENGTHEN

S1 For both Stalin and Trotsky, create a spider diagram showing their strengths in one colour and weaknesses in another.
S2 Who were Stalin's political allies and opponents in 1924, 1926 and 1928?
S3 In 1929, was Stalin a left-wing or right-wing Communist?

CHALLENGE

C1 How big a mistake do you think Lenin made in criticising all the other leaders?
C2 Given his success in the Civil War, why was Trotsky so easily defeated in the power struggle?
C3 Why do you think Stalin changed his policy outlook throughout the power struggle?

SUMMARY

- When the Bolsheviks seized power they wanted to create the world's first Communist state, although there was no agreed way of how this should be done.
- In 1924, a power struggle developed following the death of Lenin. The main contenders were Stalin, Trotsky, Kamenev, Bukharin and Zinoviev.
- Policy debates formed an important part of the power struggle. The left wing, led by Trotsky, preferred rapid industrialisation and worldwide revolution.
- The right wing, led by Bukharin, supported the NEP and socialism in one country.
- Stalin changed his views throughout the power struggle, partly for tactical reasons, but also as a response to changes in the Soviet Union's domestic and international position.
- Stalin was a clever and ruthless politician. He claimed he was Lenin's successor. He was also prepared to make and break alliances and expel his rivals.
- Stalin's biggest advantage was his position as General Secretary. He was able to fill the Party with his supporters and then win votes in crucial meetings.
- Stalin's opponents made important mistakes, including not publishing Lenin's Testament and continually underestimating Stalin.
- Although he was not the favourite to begin with, by 1929 Stalin had defeated all of his rivals and became the new leader of the Soviet Union.

EXAM GUIDANCE: PART (C) QUESTIONS

A01   **A02**

SKILLS PROBLEM SOLVING, REASONING,
DECISION MAKING, ADAPTIVE
LEARNING, INNOVATION

Question to be answered: The main reason why Stalin was undisputed leader of the Soviet Union in 1929 was Trotsky's unpopularity. How far do you agree? Explain your answer.

You may use the following in your answer:
- Trotsky's unpopularity
- Stalin's clever tactics.

You **must** also use information of your own.   (16 marks)

Analysis Question: What do I have to do to answer the question well?
- You have been given two topics on which to write: Trotsky's unpopularity and Stalin's clever tactics. You don't have to use the stimulus material provided and can use other factors. However, you will find it hard to assess the role of Trotsky's unpopularity if you don't write about it!
- You must avoid just giving the information. You have to say why the reasons you choose helped Stalin became leader of the Soviet Union.
- You are also asked to consider whether Trotsky's unpopularity was the main reason, so you are going to need to compare reasons.
- You have been given Stalin's clever tactics as another reason, but you will see that the question says you must use information of your own. So you should include at least one factor, other than those you have been given.
- In summary, to score very high marks on this question, you need to give:
  - coverage of content range (at least three factors)
  - coverage of arguments for and against the statement
  - clear reasons (criteria) for an overall judgement, backed by a convincing argument.

Answer

I mainly disagree with this view. Although it was an important reason, I think Stalin's clever tactics were more important.

Although not the main reason, Trotsky's unpopularity played a role. Trotsky should have been a strong contender in the power struggle. Lenin liked him and praised him in his Last Testament. Trotsky was also a hero because he helped organise the October 1917 seizure of power. He also led the Red Army in the Civil War. However, all these advantages were undone by Trotsky's unpopularity. People saw him as arrogant and did not like him as a person. Trotsky was criticised for not attending Lenin's funeral. This made him look as though he did not care about Lenin, which was damaging because many people in the Party worshipped Lenin. Trotsky was also unpopular because he spoke about 'permanent revolution' and many people wanted a period of calm to recover from the Civil War. As a result, few people wanted Trotsky as leader and this helped Stalin become leader instead.

Good. You have started with a short, focused introduction which provides a direct answer to the question. There is no need to write a lengthy introduction in an exam.

This is a well-written paragraph. The first sentence links to the question. The paragraph then fully explains why he was unpopular and ends by linking this material back to the outcome of the leadership struggle.

Another well-written paragraph, which tells the reader that you think clever tactics was the most important reason. You provide a range of examples, showing excellent subject knowledge.

I think the main reason was Stalin's clever tactics. Stalin was cunning and was prepared to make and break alliances in order to isolate his opponents and defeat them steadily. Stalin knew that he could not defeat Trotsky by himself. As a result he formed an alliance with Kamenev and Zinoviev. They were powerful politicians and they helped Stalin to destroy Trotsky. When this was done, Stalin formed an alliance with Bukharin to defeat Kamenev and Zinoviev. Finally, he turned on Bukharin. Stalin also used other clever tactics. He told Trotsky the wrong date of Lenin's funeral to make him look bad. At the funeral, Stalin made the main speech and portrayed himself as the person best suited to carry on Lenin's vision. As Lenin was so popular, this was a good move and Party members wanted someone who would continue Lenin's work. As a result Stalin became leader because he used a variety of clever tactics.

Good. You have provided a relevant third factor of your own. This is essential for gaining full marks.

The final reason for Stalin becoming leader was the popularity of his policies. Communist Party members wanted their new leader to have the right vision for how to build communism in the Soviet Union. They were all very interested in policies. They liked Stalin's policy of socialism in one country. This stated that the Soviet Union could build communism without the help of the developed West. This policy appealed to people's patriotism. In the late 1920s Stalin also spoke out against the New Economic Policy and said it needed to be replaced by a policy of rapid industrialisation. This was also popular because the NEP had led to high unemployment. Some business people called NEP-men had also grown rich, which was unpopular. Stalin therefore became leader because he put forward the right policies.

Your answer finishes with an evaluative conclusion, which considers the 'how far' aspect of the question.

I therefore only partly agree with the statement. Trotsky's unpopularity did play a role as it meant this powerful politician was weakened and few people wanted to support him. But this was not as important as Stalin's clever tactics, which allowed him to exploit Trotsky's unpopularity and destroy his main rivals.

What are the strengths and weaknesses of this answer?
This is an excellent answer. It explains the role of three factors in making Stalin undisputed leader and it finishes with a well-reasoned conclusion.

Answer checklist
- ☐ Identifies causes
- ☐ Provides detailed information to support the causes
- ☐ Shows how the causes led to the given outcome
- ☐ Provides a factor other than those given in the question
- ☐ Addresses 'main reason' by looking at arguments for and against, and comparing.

2. FIVE YEAR PLANS AND COLLECTIVISATION

LEARNING OBJECTIVES

☐ Understand why Stalin decided to launch the twin policies of industrialisation and collectivisation

☐ Understand how these two policies were implemented

☐ Understand the positive and negative results of industrialisation and collectivisation.

The Communists seized power in 1917 and had bold plans for the future. Many of these plans were put on hold during the moderate years of the New Economic Policy (NEP). However, in 1928, Stalin signalled the return of radicalism by plunging the Soviet Union into a vast and untried economic experiment. The impact of this 'second revolution' was extraordinary. Under a series of Five Year Plans, the Soviet Union became a chaotic building site of factories, steel mills, mines, canals, railways and power plants. A heavy industrial base was developed from almost nothing.

In the countryside, peasants were ordered to give up their land and form collective farms. The results were disastrous. Collectivisation caused a famine in which 5 million people died. Instead of experiencing modernisation and prosperity in their villages, peasants found themselves eating grass, tree bark and sometimes even their own children to survive.

For Stalin, in pursuit of a Communist paradise, this human misery was judged a price well worth paying.

2.1 STALIN AND INDUSTRIALISATION

LEARNING OBJECTIVES

▯ Understand Stalin's economic aims

▯ Understand Stalin's policy of industrialisation

▯ Understand the successes and failures of those policies.

KEY TERMS

collectivisation the organisation of agricultural land into one great area which was farmed communally by the peasants rather than them working on small individual farms

mechanised using machines instead of people or animals

In the late 1920s, Stalin began the twin economic policies of rapid industrialisation and forced **collectivisation**. As Source A shows, his aims were clear.

■ Stalin wanted to create a modern economy, based on heavy industry and a highly **mechanised** farming sector.

■ He wanted the Soviet Union's economy to be able to compete with the advanced countries of the West, and eventually overtake them.

■ He wanted to make the Soviet Union economically **self-sufficient** in order to prepare it for war.

For Stalin, these economic aims were so important that there was no time to lose. Failure, as he warned in 1931, would result in the destruction of the Soviet Union. The truth of this was seen just 10 years after he made this speech. In 1941 the Soviet Union faced invasion by around 4 million highly trained German soldiers. Thanks to Stalin, the country's economy was ready.

SOURCE A

Part of a speech made by Stalin to the First All-Union Conference of Industrial Managers, 4 February 1931.

People ask if the pace can be slackened. No! To slacken the pace would mean falling behind. And those who fall behind get beaten. Old Russia was continually beaten for her backwardness – her military, cultural, political, industrial, agricultural backwardness. That is why Lenin said on the eve of the October Revolution: 'Either perish, or overtake and outstrip the advanced capitalist countries.' We are fifty or a hundred years behind the advanced countries. We must make good this distance in ten years. Either we do it, or we shall go under.

REASONS FOR INDUSTRIALISATION

KEY TERM

ideologically based on a set of beliefs; in this case communist beliefs

Stalin had many reasons for launching his policy of rapid industrialisation.

■ Economically it seemed to offer a better alternative to the NEP.

■ **Ideologically**, it would remove class enemies and move the Soviet Union towards communism.

■ Militarily, it would prepare the country for war.

■ Politically, it promised to increase Stalin's power.

THE FAILINGS OF THE NEW ECONOMIC POLICY

In the late 1920s, the Soviet economy was based on the ideas of the New Economic Policy, first introduced by Lenin in 1921. It had the following key features.

■ Money was reintroduced.

■ Forced grain seizures from the peasants were stopped.

- Peasants could sell their surplus grain for profit.
- Small businesses and factories could be privately owned.
- Businesses could make and keep their profits.
- Only the largest industries were controlled by the state.

However, the economic performance of the NEP had been disappointing for many Communists. As the following table shows, although the economy had recovered well from the damage done by the Civil War, it had not fully caught up with the last years of Tsarism. Furthermore, the Soviet Union lay far behind the economies of the West. Even France, which was hardly regarded as a great industrial power, managed to produce more coal and steel than the Soviet Union. High rates of unemployment added to the feeling that the NEP was no longer working and needed to be replaced with a policy of rapid industrialisation.

▼ Economic performance from 1913 to 1926

	1913	1921	1926
Factory production (millions of roubles)	10,251	2,004	11,083
Coal (millions of tonnes)	29	8.9	27.6
Steel (thousands of tonnes)	4,231	183	3,141

IDEOLOGICAL REASONS

The NEP also fell out of favour on ideological grounds. It meant the Soviet Union had a **capitalist** economy, in which the factories and businesses tended to be owned by a few wealthy individuals and many workers were treated unfairly. Two groups of people who were closely identified with the NEP came to be hated by the Communists.

- Nepmen. An insult used by the Communists to describe people who had set up businesses under the NEP and become successful.
- Bourgeois experts. Another negative term invented by the Communists to describe former factory owners and managers from Tsarist times who were given jobs in the large state-owned factories. Although their skills were needed, they were strongly disliked because few of them were Communists, even though they held important positions.

Stalin's policy of rapid industrialisation promised to get rid of these class enemies. The whole economy would be taken into state hands and run for the benefit of all.

There was another ideological benefit. According to Marxist theory, communism could only exist in a highly advanced industrial nation. However, the Soviet Union was still a mainly rural land. Rapid industrialisation was therefore needed to turn peasants into workers and create a country of towns and cities, complete with mines, steelworks and factories. Only then could it advance towards full communism.

FEAR OF INVASION

The Civil War had shown how hostile the outside world was to the Soviet Union. Britain, France, the USA and Japan had all intervened on the side of the White armies. Churchill had even spoken about strangling 'Bolshevism in its cradle'. In 1927, fears of invasion returned. Three events convinced the Soviet

KEY TERM

capitalist (economy) a capitalist economy was the way the countries of the West ran their economies. It went against the principles of Communism

ACTIVITY

You are the BBC's foreign correspondent based in Moscow in 1929. Create a script for a radio broadcast explaining Stalin's decision to abandon the NEP in favour of a policy of rapid industrialisation. You could bring in experts to interview, including Stalin himself.

THE NATURE OF INDUSTRIALISATION

▼ **Figure 2.1** Central planning under the Five Year Plans

1 Gosplan decided on overall targets for each industry in the Soviet Union.

2 These overall targets were then broken down into targets for each region.

3 The regions set targets for each factory, workshop, mine, etc.

4 The managers of each industrial enterprise set targets for each foreman (the main worker in charge).

5 The foremen set targets for each shift and even individual workers.

government that the outside world was rapidly turning against them, and they decided that a Western invasion was near.

- The British government, accusing Soviet **officials** of spreading revolutionary **propaganda**, searched the Soviet trade mission in London and then broke off **diplomatic** relations.
- In China, the Communists under Mao Zedong were attacked by their political opponents, the Nationalists, resulting in a civil war.
- A Soviet diplomat (Pyotr Voykov) was assassinated in Poland.

The Communists had misunderstood the situation. There had never been any invasion threat to the Soviet Union. Nevertheless, Stalin realised that the country was dangerously unprepared for war. To defend itself, it needed to develop a heavy industrial base to produce vital materials like iron and steel. It also needed an **armaments industry** to make **tanks**, planes and ammunition. As Stalin made clear in speeches like Source A, the quicker the Soviet Union industrialised, the better. It was a matter of national survival.

POLITICAL MOTIVES

For Stalin, launching a policy of rapid industrialisation brought clear political advantages. It allowed him to divide his political opponents on the right wing of the Party, including Bukharin, thus completing his victory in the struggle to hold power. Being in charge of such a far-reaching policy also greatly improved Stalin's authority in the Party. It is no coincidence that he called it the 'second revolution'. Stalin was placing himself alongside Lenin, leader of the 'first revolution' in October 1917.

In 1924 the 'State Committee for Planning', more often called Gosplan, was a little-known government department. It had a small staff of 34 people, most of whom had backgrounds in industry rather than the Party. They produced advice on economic policy. The importance of Gosplan was transformed by Stalin's decision to turn the Soviet Union into a modern, industrial power as quickly as possible. Gosplan was given the task of creating a series of Five Year Plans (see Figure 2.1). These set out ambitious economic targets for the whole of the Soviet Union. Gosplan also developed the plans in great detail, so that even workers had individual goals.

An economy organised in this way is known as a **command economy** and it was a completely new idea. Administering the Five Year Plans was a huge task and Gosplan, based in Moscow, soon employed over half a million officials.

THE FIRST THREE FIVE YEAR PLANS

Between 1928 and 1941, there were three Five Year Plans. All had the following common features:

- Heavy industries, such as coal, oil, iron, steel and electricity, were prioritised.
- Consumer industries, which made things for ordinary people such as shoes and clothing, were overlooked.
- All of the plans were declared complete ahead of schedule.
- Although the targets were rarely met, important advances in industry were made.

▼ Overview of the three Five Year Plans

	FIRST FIVE YEAR PLAN OCTOBER 1928 TO DECEMBER 1932	SECOND FIVE YEAR PLAN JANUARY 1933 TO DECEMBER 1937	THIRD FIVE YEAR PLAN JANUARY 1938 TO JUNE 1941
Main aims	■ Expand heavy industries.	■ Expand heavy industries. ■ Develop new chemical industries. ■ Improve railway, canal and road transport links. ■ Make some consumer goods.	■ Expand heavy industries. ■ Armaments production.
Successes	■ The economy grew by a huge 14 per cent each year. ■ Coal and iron output doubled. ■ Steel production increased by one-third.	■ More realistic targets were set. ■ Big advances continued to be made in heavy industry. ■ Other important areas of the economy started to be developed. ■ Gains were made in chemical industries such as fertiliser production. ■ New transport schemes such as the Moscow Metro and Moscow canal were completed.	■ By 1940, one-third of government investment was spent on defence. ■ The basis of a powerful arms industry was laid. ■ Nine new aircraft factories were established.
Weaknesses	■ Many targets were not met. ■ Targets were set at unrealistic levels. ■ Many factories struggled to obtain the necessary resources. ■ There was a lack of skilled workers. ■ Living and working standards declined dramatically. ■ Many products were of extremely poor quality.	■ Despite promises to raise living standards, consumer industries received little investment.	■ The Plan ran into difficulties because Stalin's purges led to the arrest of many experienced factory managers and Gosplan officials. ■ The Plan was cut short by the Nazi invasion of Russia in June 1941.

EXTEND YOUR KNOWLEDGE

The high growth rates achieved under the first Five Year Plan seem even more impressive when compared to the rest of the world at the time. Many countries were in the grip of an economic depression, caused by the collapse of the Wall Street stock market in 1929. In the USA, for example, industrial production had fallen by around 40 per cent by 1932 and unemployment was 25 per cent.

KEY TERM

rations a fixed amount of something that people are allowed when there is not enough

STAKHANOVITES

For many workers, being part of the Five Year Plans gave their lives a sense of excitement and purpose. This was helped by a massive propaganda campaign. Posters like Source B celebrated their efforts. One of the cleverest but most controversial propaganda campaigns focused on the efforts of a miner called Alexei Stakhanov.

In August 1935, Stakhanov mined 102 tonnes of coal in 6 hours. This was 14 times the output of a normal miner. He was rewarded with 1 month's wages, a new apartment and a holiday. He also became the centre of a huge publicity campaign promoting 'the Stakhanovite Movement'.

■ Propaganda posters and news reports held him up as a model Soviet worker.
■ Statues were built in his honour.
■ Stakhanov toured the country, encouraging other workers to follow his example.
■ Workers were promised rewards such as a new flat, higher wages or bigger **rations** if they managed to exceed their targets like Stakhanov.

SOURCE B

'The Reality of our Program is Real People: It's You and Me'. A 1931 Soviet propaganda poster.

ACTIVITY

1 What do you think the poster in Source B is saying?
2 What different views might Soviet workers have about its message?

As a result of the Stakhanov Movement, many people were encouraged to work harder. Within a year, almost one-quarter of industrial workers were categorised as Stakhanovites. But this also created difficulties. 'Recordmania' occurred and managers had to spend a lot of time dealing with attempts to set new production records. This disrupted normal working patterns. Other workers did not like the pressure on them to work harder. Some Stakhanovite workers were even attacked. The word 'Stakhanovite' soon came to mean a pushy person who was more interested in helping themselves rather than their colleagues.

In the 1980s, the Communist Party finally admitted the truth behind Stakhanov's amazing achievement. It had been a publicity stunt. Instead of working alone, Stakhanov had been supported by a team of fellow miners. The authorities had also provided him with state-of-the-art equipment.

SOURCE C

Alexei Stakhanov at the coal face, passing on tips to a fellow miner.

ACTIVITY

1 Why do you think the Soviet government decided to lie to its people about Stakhanov's achievements?
2 In what other ways was there a culture of lying under Stalin's rule?

EXAM-STYLE QUESTION

A04

SKILLS ANALYSIS, INTERPRETATION, CREATIVITY

Study Extract A. What impression does the author give about the first Five Year Plan? You must use Extract A to explain your answer.   **(6 marks)**

EXTRACT A

From a book about Stalin's rule, published in in 1995.

In 1930 work began on a dam on the Ural River to supply the steel factory in Magnitogorsk with water. There was competition between left and right river banks: 'Everyone to the dam! Everything for the dam!' The dam was built in a record 74 days, well ahead of schedule. One contemporary writer wrote: 'The Magnitogorsk dam was the school at which people began to respect Communist miracles.' But it was not deep enough and the water froze, and a new dam five times as big was started almost immediately. When it was completed the first dam was submerged.

HINT

To do well in this question, look at the evidence selected by the author. Can you see a viewpoint being made deliberately?

SUCCESS AND FAILURES OF INDUSTRIALISATION

By 1941, the Soviet Union had been transformed from a mainly agricultural society into a powerful industrial nation. In a speech in 1933, Stalin proudly set out the achievements of his policy (Source D).

SOURCE D

Stalin speaking about the first Five Year Plans in 1933.

We did not have an iron and steel industry, the basis for the industrialisation of the country. Now we have one.

We did not have a tractor industry. Now we have one.

We did not have an automobile industry. Now we have one.

We did not have a machine-tool industry. Now we have one.

We did not have a big and modern chemical industry. Now we have one.

We did not have a real and big industry for the production of modern agricultural machinery. Now we have one.

We did not have an aircraft industry. Now we have one.

In output of electric power we were last on the list. Now we rank among the first.

In output of oil products and coal we were last on the list. Now we rank among the first.

SUCCESSES OF INDUSTRIALISATION

The successes of industrialisation covered several aspects:
■ Heavy industry was the biggest success. As the table on the following page shows, in the space of 12 years, oil output had more than doubled, and coal, iron, electricity and steel production had multiplied.
■ Advances were made in transport. There was a large expansion of the railway and canal networks, allowing goods to be transported more efficiently.

- The Five Year Plans created a modern armaments industry. These factories and the weapons they produced were crucial in defeating Nazi Germany in the Second World War.
- The Plans increased the size of the working class and turned the Soviet Union into a more urbanised society.
- There were some gains for the workers. Unemployment vanished. Cheap meals were provided in factory canteens. Those workers lucky enough to be categorised as Stakhanovites benefited from improved wages and living conditions.

EXTEND YOUR KNOWLEDGE

Under the Five Year Plans, many factories were built in areas that had never previously been industrialised, including Siberia, the Ural Mountains and central Asia. When Nazi Germany invaded the Soviet Union, these factories were out of range of German bomber aircraft and could continue producing vast numbers of tanks, guns and aircraft. This helped the Soviet Union to defeat Nazi Germany.

▼ Industrial output during the first three Five Year Plans. These figures are based on Soviet sources and so cannot be considered completely accurate

	▼ 1927	▼ 1932	▼ 1937	▼ 1940
Coal (millions of tonnes)	35	64	128	150
Steel (millions of tonnes)	3	6	18	18
Oil (millions of tonnes)	12	21	26	26
Electricity (million kWH)	18	20	80	90

ACTIVITY

1 Use the table to work out the percentage growth rates in each industry between 1927 and 1940.
2 Which industries did particularly well?
3 Do you think any industries would have concerned the Soviet authorities?

KEY TERM

showpiece project special project like the Moscow underground, designed to impress the rest of the world

The three Five Year Plans included many **showpiece projects**, designed to prove that communism was better than capitalism (see Figure 2.2). Stalin's obsession with big schemes has been referred to as 'Giganto-mania'.

THE FAILURES OF INDUSTRIALISATION
Despite what Stalin was telling the people, there was another side to industrialisation. The Five Year Plans were often delivered at enormous cost to workers, and the supposed successes were highly exaggerated.

- The quality of goods produced in the factories was very low. This was because the Plans set targets for quantity, not quality, and so this was all that factory managers focused on.
- There were high levels of waste. Lack of transport as well as poor organisation and planning meant that items produced by factories were often stored on site and allowed to decay, rather than being used.
- Most of the targets set by Gosplan were unrealistically high. Factory managers were under huge pressure to meet their targets, and often turned to bribery and sometimes outright theft in order to obtain vital supplies for their factories. Failure to meet production targets could result in imprisonment.

▲ **Figure 2.2** The major achievements of Stalin's three Five Year Plans

❶ Chelisbinsk. A major tractor producing centre. By 1940 it had turned out around 100,000 tractors.

❷ Gorky. An important centre of motor vehicle manufacturing.

❸ Magnitogorsk. A new city and site of the Soviet Union's largest steel plant.

❹ Novosibirsk. An important location for the building of machine tools.

❺ Stalingrad. A centre of heavy industry. By 1939 its 'Red October' tractor works was producing half the tractors in the Soviet Union.

❻ The White Sea Canal. A 227 km waterway connecting the White Sea to the Baltic Sea. It was built in just 20 months.

❼ Moscow–Donetsk Railway. An important railway line, connecting the capital with Ukraine.

❽ Built by 75,000 workers, the first line of the Moscow Metro was opened in 1935. Its stations were elaborately designed and it was seen as a showpiece of Soviet achievement.

❾ Moscow–Volga Canal. An important 128 km waterway, connecting the capital with Europe's longest river, the Volga. This meant goods could be more easily moved through central and southern Russia.

❿ Trans-Siberian Railway. Originally constructed between 1891 and 1914, 7,000 km of track were modernised under the second Five Year Plan.

⓫ Dnieper Dam. At 61 metres high and stretching 800 metres across the River Dnieper, it was the world's largest hydro-electric dam on its opening in 1932.

■ Lying about production figures was common. To avoid arrest, factory managers tended to exaggerate successes and hide failures. Gosplan officials at the regional level were under similar pressure to exceed their targets and so would falsely increase production levels. A similar process would happen with the top officials in Moscow. As a result, official Soviet statistics were extremely unreliable.

■ Some of the showpiece projects started under the Five Year Plans relied on forced labour. The White Sea Canal, for example, was built by 100,000 prisoners from the Gulags. Around 12,000 died during construction.

- Overall, the Plans gave little thought to improving the lives of ordinary workers (see Chapter 4). With millions of peasants pouring into the towns and cities, a housing shortage developed.
- Between 1928 and 1941, there were continuous shortages of consumer goods, such as clothes, shoes and furniture. This was because Stalin prioritised heavy industry and defence. Standing for hours in shop queues became a feature of everyday life.
- Working conditions were very difficult. Seven-day working weeks and long hours were common. Basic safety standards were ignored, so accidents at work were frequent. Under the third Five Year Plan, internal passports were introduced to stop workers moving from town to town in search of better-paid jobs.

SOURCE E

The largest blast furnace in the Soviet Union under construction at Magnitogorsk.

MAGNITOGORSK

The construction of the vast steelworks and new city at Magnitogorsk highlights both the success and failures of Stalin's industrialisation drive. The site chosen couldn't have been more difficult. It was a remote, uninhabited area next to a mountain with unusually high levels of iron ore, leading to the plant's name, Magnetic Mountain. The first **shock workers** arrived in March 1929 to begin breaking the ground. By 1932, there were 250,000 workers were on site and steel production had begun.

Magnitogorsk became a symbol of Soviet achievement and the story of its construction was publicised throughout the Soviet Union. But the propaganda did not mention that a significant amount of the steel it produced was of poor quality. Nor did it focus on the grim reality of everyday life. The initial promise of building a bright, clean Socialist city of the future was never realised. The majority of workers lived in mud huts, wooden shacks and tents, with no heating or bathroom facilities. Conditions were so hard that the average workers stayed for just 82 days. These were the lucky ones. Magnitogorsk could not have been built without the labour of 40,000 political prisoners.

'The main effect of Stalin's three Five Year Plans on the Soviet Union in the years 1928–41 was the rapid development of Soviet industry.' Do you agree?

You may use the following in your answer:
- the development of Soviet industry
- transport links.

You **must** also use information of your own. **(16 marks)**

2.2 STALIN AND COLLECTIVISATION

LEARNING OBJECTIVES

Understand Stalin's policy of collectivisation

Understand opposition to collectivisation and how it was overcome

Understand the successes and failures of those policies.

The Soviet Union was founded on the idea of an alliance between the urban workers and peasantry. Lenin called it the *smychka* (meaning collaboration in society, or union) and it is why the Soviet Union's flag contained a hammer (signifying the workers) and sickle (a farming tool, the symbol of the villagers). In 1929, Stalin introduced a major change to how agriculture had been organised under Lenin's New Economic Policy. Peasants were forced to give up their privately owned land and form it into large-scale, state-controlled farms. Stalin had many reasons for collectivising agriculture.

■ Economically, he wanted to modernise an old-fashioned farming system. He also wanted a guaranteed supply of grain in order to feed the workers and to sell it abroad to pay for industrialisation.

■ Ideologically, Stalin, like many Communists, believed that peasants were not really supporters of communism. So he wanted to change the way farming was organised to ensure they followed true communist methods.

■ Politically, Stalin wanted to extend Communist control over the countryside. He also saw this policy as a way of weakening his opponent, Bukharin, in the struggle for power.

ECONOMIC REASONS

Stalin believed that collectivisation was necessary in order to modernise the Soviet Union's inefficient and outdated farming system. Although there were some exceptions, most farms in the 1920s were small and often divided into strips, similar to English farming in the Middle Ages. Most crops were sown and harvested by hand. Machinery such as tractors and **combine harvesters** were rarely used, and chemical fertilisers to boost crop production were almost unknown. This meant that farm output in the 1920s was so low that food shortages were a constant problem.

Stalin saw collectivisation as the solution. Because **collective** farms would be much larger, modern machinery could be used. These, it was planned, would be supplied by the state through huge Motor Tractor Stations. Experts would also teach peasants to farm in more modern ways. The result would be big increases in food production. This in turn would aid the drive to industrialise in three ways.

1 The workers in towns and cities would be well fed.

2 The government could sell more food abroad to pay for expensive foreign technology.

3 By mechanising the farms, fewer people would be needed to work on the land. This would release valuable labour to work in the new factories.

IDEOLOGICAL REASONS

Collectivisation was a key part of Stalin's mission to build communism across the Soviet Union. Just like in the cities, Stalin believed that the NEP was pushing the country in the wrong ideological direction.

This was because the NEP encouraged peasants to behave like capitalists:

■ They were allowed to own property.
■ They could sell their produce for profit.
■ If they were rich enough, they could employ landless labourers to work on their land.

The Communists argued that class divisions had developed in the countryside (see Figure 2.3) and they identified the **kulaks** as their major enemy.

▶ **Figure 2.3** The different classes of peasant during the New Economic Policy

Kulaks
Better-off peasants who owned enough land to make a reasonable living and live in a more comfortable house. In Russian, 'kulak' means 'fist' or 'grasping' and reveals how less well-off peasants in the villages resented the richer peasants.

Middle peasants
Owned a small amount of land and lived in the villages.

Poor peasants
Did not own any land. Hired themselves out as labourers on the farms of their wealthier neighbours.

Collectivisation seemed to offer a good way of building communist values in the countryside.

■ Because private landownership would be abolished, everyone would be of the same status.
■ As all the produce would go to the state, peasants would no longer be motivated by the desire to make money. They would instead be working for the good of the nation.
■ Instead of working on individual farms, peasants would learn to work together.
■ Collective farms would have shared facilities, such as canteens and gyms. These would develop a community outlook.

POLITICAL REASONS

Collectivisation was partly about political power. Firstly for Stalin, opposing the NEP and supporting collectivisation was one way of gaining the upper hand in the power struggle against Bukharin.

Secondly, it was about power for the Communist Party. While it was strong in the towns and cities of Russia, it had little control over what went on in the countryside – there were simply not enough party workers to govern such a vast area. This lack of control scared the Communists. Collectivisation was one way of enforcing their authority over the countryside.

THE GRAIN PROCUREMENT CRISIS

KEY TERM

grain procurement the policy of buying or seizing essential farm produce from the peasants in order to feed the workers in towns and cities

The short-term cause of collectivisation was the **grain procurement** crisis of 1927–28. The government found that it could not buy enough grain to feed the urban workers. The reasons for the grain shortage were as follows.

■ The peasants had reduced grain production because of the low prices being paid by the state.
■ Some farmers were withholding their grain from the market in order to push prices up.

The result was rationing in the cities. Many in the Party now turned against the peasants. One solution, of course, would have been to pay the peasants more

▲ **Figure 2.4** The Communist vision of a collective farm and farming under the NEP

ACTIVITY

Study the two pictures in Figure 2.4 carefully. Note down as many differences as you can between the two farming systems.

for their grain. However, there was little desire in the Party for this expensive approach. Stalin demonstrated this new determined mood by travelling to the Urals and Western Siberia in 1928 and supervising the forced seizure of grain. But this was just a stop-gap measure. A permanent solution was needed to guarantee the regular flow of grain to the cities, and collectivisation seemed to be the answer. It would place the state in control of the farms, and with it the grain supply.

THE NATURE OF COLLECTIVISATION

In December 1929, Stalin called for a policy of all-out collectivisation. As Source F shows, the Communists liked to show this as a **voluntary** process. Party officials, they claimed, would go into the villages and tell the peasants about the advantages of joining a collective farm. A vote would then be held, in which the villages would willingly agree to combine their farms.

SOURCE F

Official Soviet photograph showing peasants voluntarily voting to join a collective farm.

This approach rarely worked. Most peasants had no wish to collectivise. They wanted to work their own individual farms in their own way. They had no wish to be told what to grow and what animals to breed. Wild rumours also stated that collectivisation would lead to the sharing of wives and beds.

Instead of agreeing to go into collective farms, the majority of peasants rebelled. They disrupted collective farm meetings and attacked Party officials. Rather than hand over their property, many peasants set fire to their farms, and killed and ate their animals. The result was nearly civil war in the countryside. Stalin was forced to send in the army and secret police to enforce his policy violently.

OPPOSITION OF AND REMOVAL OF THE KULAKS

The majority of peasants objected to collectivisation, but the biggest objection came from those with the most to lose: the kulaks. They had worked hard under

SOURCE G

An anti-kulak propaganda poster from the early 1930s. The slogan at the top of the second reads: 'The Kulak is the Worst Enemy of Poor Peasants'. The box below it says, 'No Place for Kulaks in Complete Collectivisation Regions'.

the NEP and made enough money to buy additional farm land and sometimes even hire workers. As Source H shows, they were not prepared to give this up without a fight. However it would be wrong to see the kulaks as a wealthy elite. Most were only slightly richer than the average peasant. This small difference did not matter to the Communists. They believed the kulaks were a dangerous class enemy. In their propaganda, kulaks were shown as greedy capitalists, who occupied all the best land and exploited the poorer peasants. They also selfishly hid grain in order to increase food prices while the workers went hungry. In 1929, Stalin gave a shocking order: 'Liquidate the kulaks as a class.'

SOURCE H

From an account by a Communist Party official, who took part in the collectivisation process.

So this was 'Liquidation of the evil kulaks as a class!' A lot of simple peasants being torn from their native soil, stripped of their worldly goods and shipped to some distant labour camps. Their outcries filled the air. As I stood there, distressed, ashamed, helpless, I heard a woman shouting in an unearthly voice... The woman held a flaming sheaf of grain in her hands. Before anyone could reach her, she had tossed the burning sheaf of grain into the thatched roof of the house, which burst into flames. 'Infidels! Murderers!' the distraught woman was shrieking. 'We worked all our lives for our house. You won't have it. The flames will have it.'

Kulaks were forbidden from joining collective farms. Instead they were rounded up by dekulakisation squads, made up of army units, secret police and gangs of loyal party members from the cities. Soon, however, the term 'kulak' lost any real meaning, as it was applied to anyone who opposed collectivisation, rich or poor. The numbers involved in the dekulakisation drive rapidly escalated. Thousands were simply shot on the spot. Around 2 million were loaded onto cattle trucks, transported to Siberia and imprisoned in forced labour camps run by the secret police. Others were exiled closer to home, but on land deliberately chosen as it was too poor to farm.

KOLKHOZES AND MOTOR TRACTOR STATIONS

After the brutal process of collectivisation, the peasants' new reality became either the state farm (*sovkhoz* in Russian) or the kolkhoz, meaning collective farm. The state farms tended to be far larger than the collective farms. The peasants who worked on them were treated as 'outdoor workers' and paid a fixed wage by the government.

Most peasants ended up working on a collective farm. By 1940, 240,000 kolkhozes had been created across Russia. A typical kolkhoz had the following features.

■ They were made up of 50–100 families.
■ Each kolkhoz was run by a chairman, who was a Communist Party member from the town.
■ The hours the peasants worked and their jobs were set by the state.
■ The state decided what was to be grown and supplied the equipment.
■ The majority of the kolkhoz produce was taken by the state for a fixed low price.
■ This money was then shared out among the peasants. The peasants were very badly paid.
■ Peasants were not allowed to leave the kolkhoz to work in the towns.
■ After 1935, peasants were given a small area of land to farm for themselves, on which they could also keep a limited number of farm animals.

ACTIVITY

Read Source H carefully.
1 What can we learn from this source about collectivisation?
2 Did anything in this source surprise you? If so, why?

EXTEND YOUR KNOWLEDGE

In Soviet propaganda, kolkhozes were shown as large, modern units. The reality was very different. The average kolkhoz was based on the old village. It contained 76 families who lived in the same houses as before, and had only 60 cattle, 94 sheep and goats, and 26 pigs.

As part of the **modernisation** drive, Motor Tractor Stations (MTSs) were set up to rent out farm machinery to groups of collective farms. By 1940 there was one MTS for every 40 collective farms. However, the stations had a number of weaknesses. They never had enough tractors to meet demand. The tractors were often unreliable because they were badly built in the first place and then badly maintained; the 'mechanics' tended to be peasants who lacked the necessary skills. It was also expensive to hire the machinery, and this put off some collective farms. As a result, traditional farming methods, such as harvesting by hand and using the horse-drawn plough, continued to be used.

The MTSs became hated by many peasants because the officials running them were responsible for ensuring the collective farms handed over their grain **quotas**. In addition, each MTS had a political department. Its job was to spread Communist propaganda and to spy on the peasants. Trouble-makers on the farms could be arrested very quickly.

SOURCE I

A Soviet joke from the 1930s.

Q: How do you deal with mice in the Kremlin?

A: Put up a sign saying 'collective farm'. Then half the mice will starve, and the rest will run away.

SUCCESS AND FAILURES OF COLLECTIVISATION

By 1935, over 90 per cent of Soviet farmland was collectivised. Despite peasant opposition, collectivisation did bring benefits to the Soviet Union, and to Stalin personally. These successes, however, came at a cost.

▼ Agricultural production in the Soviet Union. These figures are based on Soviet sources and so cannot be considered completely accurate

	▼ 1928	▼ 1929	▼ 1930	▼ 1931	▼ 1932	▼ 1933
Grain harvest (millions of tonnes)	73.3	71.7	83.5	69.5	69.6	68.4
State procurement of grain (millions of tonnes)	10.8	16.1	22.1	22.8	18.5	22.6
Grain exports (millions of tonnes)	0.3	0.18	4.76	5.06	1.73	1.69
Cattle (million per head)	70.5	67.1	52.3	47.9	40.1	38.4
Pigs (million per head)	26.0	20.1	13.6	14.4	11.6	12.1

EXTEND YOUR KNOWLEDGE

The table above shows that although state procurement levels went up between 1928 and 1933, the state always procured considerably less grain than the full harvest. This was because the collective farms had to hand over a large proportion of their harvest to the MTS as payment for the use of machinery. Grain had to be kept for seed and animal feed. A small portion was also distributed to the collective farmers themselves.

ACTIVITY

How well can you 'spin' the statistics?
1 Take on the role of a Gosplan official. **Compile** a short report for the public, emphasising the successes of collectivisation.
2 Write a second report from an exiled opponent who has got hold of the same figures. What critical remarks could they make?

FAILURES OF COLLECTIVISATION

The short-term impact of collectivisation was a collapse in food production. As the above table highlights, between 1928 and 1933, grain harvests fell by 7 per cent. Falls in livestock were more dramatic – cattle numbers almost halved. Although this did not cause famine in the cities, the standard of living for urban workers dropped sharply. The amount of meat they ate fell by two-thirds, for example. After 1935, grain production began slowly to recover, but it took 20 years for animal numbers to regain their pre-collectivisation levels.

In the medium to long term, Stalin's hopes of creating a modern, highly productive farming system never emerged. This was because of the following:
- The Motor Tractor Stations did not have enough machinery. What little they had tended to be badly maintained and expensive to hire.
- Dekulakisation had removed the most skilled and productive farmers.
- Above all, productivity was poor. As the peasants did not own the land they worked on and were very poorly paid, they had no reason to work hard. Instead they did just enough to avoid being fined.
- Instead of working hard on the collective farms, peasants put most of their energy into their small private plots. Making up just 4 per cent of the farmed area, they supplied the majority of the Soviet Union's vegetables, fruit, meat and milk.
- Despite countless attempts at reform by later Soviet leaders, the collective farms system remained a major area of weakness in the Soviet economy.

THE GREAT FAMINE, 1932–33

Collectivisation contributed to a widespread famine in 1932–33. Although exact numbers are not known, estimates suggest that 4–5 million people died.

The hardest-hit region was Ukraine. Despite being known as Europe's 'breadbasket' because of its vast, rich farmland, millions of Ukrainians died from starvation. To survive, people ate earthworms, tree bark, mice, ants and even human flesh. The Soviet **regime** printed posters declaring: 'To eat your own children is a barbarian act', but more than 2,500 people were convicted of cannibalism after eating dead bodies.

In Ukraine, the famine is known as the Holodomor, which means 'extermination by hunger'. Its causes are many, and include a long drought and the chaos caused by collectivisation. Animals were killed in huge numbers and the most experienced farmers were deported. The new collective farms were badly run, as most managers came from the towns and had no experience of farming. The peasants, bitter about losing their land, put little effort into their work, including the crucial tasks of sowing seeds in spring and harvesting in autumn.

For all these reasons, food production in Ukraine, like the rest of Russia, fell rapidly in the period 1932–33. These years would have been difficult anyway, but a famine developed because of what the state did next. Even though agricultural output was reduced, grain quotas taken by the state were raised to unrealistic levels. When the quotas were not met, Stalin claimed it was deliberate **sabotage**. Communist officials from the towns, supported by the army and secret police, headed into the villages and took all the food they could find, leaving the peasants with nothing.

When famine set in, instead of giving help, the state continued its policy of brutal food seizures. If peasants were found hiding even one or two ears of corn, they were exiled or shot. Military checkpoints were set up to prevent starving

KEY TERM

sabotage to secretly damage or destroy something so that it cannot be used

A statue, named the 'Bitter Memory of Childhood,' and dedicated to the child victims of the Ukrainian famine. It is located in the National Museum 'Memorial to Holodomor victims', Kiev, Ukraine.

peasants from leaving the famine-hit areas. Publicly, Stalin's government denied there was any problem and refused offers of foreign aid. Meanwhile, as the table of agricultural production showed, grain continued to be sent abroad.

The Holodomor was a man-made tragedy. Some historians suggest that Stalin deliberately caused it for political purposes. He wanted to punish the peasantry for their heavy resistance to collectivisation. He also saw it as a way of breaking the spirit of the Ukrainian people. Ukraine had its own distinctive culture and many of its people wished for independence outside of the Soviet Union. Famine was Stalin's way of ensuring this did not happen.

EXTEND YOUR KNOWLEDGE

WAS THE UKRAINIAN FAMINE GENOCIDE?
Genocide is defined by the United Nations as an attempt 'to destroy, in whole or in part, a national, ethnical, racial or religious group'. Academics and political leaders are divided over whether the Holodomor should be classed as a genocide. Those who believe it should argue that Stalin used starvation as a deliberate weapon to terrorise the Ukrainians into obedience. Opponents point out that millions of non-Ukrainians also died in the famine, and so it cannot be seen as an attack on only one national group.

SUCCESSES OF COLLECTIVISATION

Despite its clear horrors and chaos, for Stalin collectivisation was economically a success. By taking over all the farms, the state managed to secure a guaranteed supply of grain. This was then used to:
- feed the workers in the towns and cities – by 1934, rationing of bread and many other foods ended
- sell abroad, to pay for new industrial equipment.

As a result, although the decline in grain production no doubt worried Stalin, he was much more interested in grain procurement levels. As the table earlier shows, these increased notably on 1928 levels (although less so in 1932).

Collectivisation also delivered another resource vital to industrialisation: people. Over 19 million peasants had moved to the cities. Once there, they supplied much-needed labour for the new factories.

Politically there were positives for Stalin. The decision to abandon the NEP and launch collectivisation was an important reason for Stalin's defeat of Bukharin in the power struggle.

The countryside was under total Communist control for the first time. The violence of collectivisation, combined with the famine, destroyed the independent spirit of the peasantry. Meanwhile, everyday life on collective farms involved close monitoring.
- The Motor Tractor Stations were used to monitor the countryside and spread Communist propaganda.
- The collective farms were run by members of the Communist Party.
- A system of internal passports meant peasants could not leave their farms unless they had official permission.

It is no surprise that many peasants complained of a '**second serfdom**'.

KEY TERM

second serfdom until the late 19th century, many peasants in Russia were owned by landlords and called serfs. The lack of basic freedoms led many peasants in the 1920s to draw comparisons with their own situation

Finally, it was an ideological victory. Stalin had taken a significant step towards building his vision of Communism. By 1936, 90 per cent of farms had been collectivised. Two key elements of capitalism – private land ownership and private enterprise – had therefore been largely removed from the countryside. In addition, by removing the kulaks, class divisions were ended.

▼ The 'balance sheet' for collectivisation

FAILURES	SUCCESSES
■ Two million peasants were deported to Siberia.	■ A guaranteed grain supply was secured to feed the towns.
■ Five million peasants died in the Great Famine.	■ Grain was exported to help pay for industrialisation.
■ The most ambitious farmers were lost.	■ Peasants moved to towns and cities and became workers.
■ Grain harvests fell.	■ The Communist Party gained control over the countryside.
■ Livestock numbers did not recover until the 1950s.	■ Stalin increased his political power.
■ The MTSs did not provide enough tractors.	■ Communism was created in the countryside.
■ Collective farms were unproductive.	■ Private land ownership was abolished.
	■ Class divisions were removed.

SOURCE K

A government poster from the 1930s showing the benefits of collectivisation, compared to the outdated methods of the NEP. It was entitled 'Day of harvest and collectivisation'.

ACTIVITY

Imagine that a Communist official from the local MTS and a collective farm worker were seeing the poster in Source K for the first time. Plan out a possible conversation between the two. What would they say to each other about farming in the 1920s, and about how they think collectivisation had worked out?

EXAM-STYLE QUESTION

A01   **A02**

Explain **two** effects on the Soviet Union of Stalin's decision to abandon the New Economic Policy in 1928. **(8 marks)**

HINT

To do well in this question, you need to include accurate and relevant historical information to prove your points.

RECAP

RECALL QUESTIONS

1 Which organisation was in charge of the Five Year Plans?
2 How long did the first Five Year Plan last?
3 What sector of industry did all three Five Year Plans prioritise?
4 Why did the third Five Year Plan last only 3.5 years?
5 Why did Alexei Stakhanov become a household name in the Soviet Union?
6 Which group of people did the Communist Party identify as their main enemy in the countryside?
7 What was a collective farm known as?
8 How many collective farms had been created by 1940?
9 Which region was hit particularly hard by the Great Famine?
10 What happened to grain procurement levels between 1928 and 1933?

CHECKPOINT

STRENGTHEN

S1 Note down four reasons why Stalin was not happy with the Soviet economy under the NEP.
S2 Produce a two-sentence definition of each of the following terms: Gosplan; Five Year Plans; collectivisation; Motor Tractor Station.
S3 Find four statistics that show that Stalin's economic policies were successful. Then find four statistics that show them to be a failure.

CHALLENGE

C1 Was there one main reason why Stalin wanted to industrialise the Soviet Union?
C2 Create a spider diagram showing the economic, political and social effects of both collectivisation and rapid industrialisation.
C3 'An industrial success but an agricultural failure'. Do you agree with this view of the Five Year Plans and collectivisation?

SUMMARY

- Stalin aimed to turn the Soviet Union into a modern, industrial country, with an up-to-date farming system.
- He began a policy of rapid industrialisation to get the country ready for war and because he saw it as a way of moving towards full communism.
- To industrialise the Soviet Union as quickly as possible, Gosplan created three Five Year Plans, setting out ambitious economic targets for the economy.
- Heavy industry was the main priority of the Five Year Plans. Impressive gains were made in iron, steel, coal, oil and electricity production.
- For ordinary workers, life was very tough under the Five Year Plans. Industries that made things for ordinary people received little investment.
- To make people work harder, workers were encouraged to copy the example of Stakhanov.
- In order to support the process of industrialisation, from 1928 Stalin ordered all farms to be collectivised.
- Collectivisation was a deeply unpopular policy, and many peasants resisted by killing their livestock and burning their farms.
- Collectivisation came at a huge cost. Millions were deported or died in the Great Famine. Farm production fell.
- Stalin saw collectivisation as successful, mainly because the state gained a guaranteed supply of grain.

EXAM GUIDANCE: PART (A) QUESTIONS

Study Extract A.

EXTRACT A

From a history of the Soviet Union published in 2008.

Although production had increased, many of the official targets were never met. However, large-scale fraud on the part of local administrators allowed Stalin to claim that the Plan had been 'over-fulfilled'. Local Party officials who failed to meet their production targets were demoted, sacked, or in some cases put on trial and executed as enemies of the state. Under enormous pressure, many local administrators lied about the amount of raw materials that they had been able to produce, creating the impression that targets had been exceeded. Nonetheless, in reality, few production targets were actually achieved.

AO4

SKILLS ANALYSIS, INTERPRETATION, CREATIVITY

Question to be answered: What impression does the author give about the overall success of Stalin's first Five Year Plan?

You must use Extract A to explain your answer.   (6 marks)

1   **Analysis Question 1: What is the question type testing?**
In this question, you have to make an inference from what the extract says to show what impression the author set out to create. The key to analysing the extracts is to understand that the author deliberately chooses how they write. They will make a choice about what language to use, what tone to adopt and what content to include to create an impression.

2   **Analysis Question 2: What do I have to do to answer the question well?**
Obviously you have to read the extract carefully and work out what the author is trying to make you think. Has the author set out to give a positive or negative impression, or have they set out to suggest that an event/policy or movement was significant/ineffective, successful/unsuccessful? The language and tone of the source will help you see this. Are there any especially 'emotional' words? Has the author deliberately included things or left things out?

3   **Analysis Question 3: Are there any techniques I can use to make it very clear that I am doing what is needed to be successful?**
This is a 6-mark question and you need to make sure you leave enough time to answer the other two questions fully (they are worth 22 marks in total). Therefore, you want to answer this question as quickly as you can. A good way to do this is to answer the question straight away.

You could begin with:
'The impression the author is trying to give about the overall success of the first Five Year Plan is…'

You now have to prove it. A good way to do this is to say:
'I think this because of the language and tone…'

(You can then quote Extract A to prove what you are saying about language and tone.)
'I also think this is true because of the content the author has chosen….'

(You can then quote Extract A to prove what you are saying about content choice. For example, the author creates a bad impression by not talking about the achievements of the first Five Year Plan.)

Answer A

The author gives the impression that the Five Year Plans were not very successful. I think this because of the language and tone of the extract.

What are the strengths and weaknesses of Answer A?
It correctly identifies the overall impression of the extract. However, it needs to back up the statement with evidence from the extract.

Answer B

The author suggests that the Five Year Plans were overall a failure. I think this because the author brings in a lot of evidence to support this negative view. The extract talks about 'few production targets' being met, and about how officials had to try to cover up their failings by lying. This suggests that despite the official claims, the economy was not that successful. I also think this because the tone of the source is negative. The author used words like 'failed', 'sacked', 'demoted' and 'few', which create an impression of things going wrong.

What are the strengths and weaknesses of Answer B?
This is a very good answer. It has identified the overall impression of the source and provided plenty of evidence from the source to explain this.

Challenge a friend

Use the Student Book to find a source to set a part (a) question for a friend. Then look at their answer. Does it do the following things?

☐ State a valid impression from the source
☐ Provide at least 3–4 lines explaining how language, tone and content choice prove this.

If it does, you can tell your friend that the answer is very good!

3. PURGES, SHOW TRIALS, THE CULT OF STALIN AND THE REVISION OF HISTORY

LEARNING OBJECTIVES

I Understand why Stalin carried out the purges

I Understand the key features of the purges and their impact on the Soviet Union

I Understand how propaganda and censorship were used to increase Stalin's power.

Nikolai Bukharin was first introduced in Chapter 1. In the 1920s he was a young, intelligent and good-natured politician. Lenin even called him the Party's 'golden boy'. Following defeat in the leadership struggle, Bukharin kept his personal popularity – but he was not safe. In February 1937, he was arrested and charged with attempting to overthrow the Soviet state. Although the accusations were ridiculous, he eventually admitted guilt in order to save his young wife and baby son. While awaiting his death sentence, Bukharin wrote a note to Stalin: 'Koba, why do you need me to die?' 'Koba' was one of Stalin's old revolutionary names and showed how close they had once been. It made no difference – 2 days later, Bukharin was shot.

Bukharin was one of the estimated 8 million victims of Stalin's purges. The vast majority were innocent of any crime, but they were executed or imprisoned because of Stalin's need for absolute power. However, being obeyed out of fear was not enough for Stalin. He wanted to be admired and loved. To achieve this, the whole cultural life of the Soviet Union – the work of journalists, writers, artists and musicians – was used to build a cult of personality around him. People were repeatedly told that Stalin was a kind, fatherly figure leading them to a great future. Most people ended up believing this.

3.1 THE REASONS FOR THE PURGES

LEARNING OBJECTIVES

- Understand how Kirov's murder helped lead to the purges
- Understand how Stalin's desire for total control was a key reason for the purges
- Understand how economics and Lenin's legacy both contributed to the purges.

KEY TERM

Old Bolsheviks the name given to highly respected Party members who had worked alongside Lenin and participated in the revolutionary struggle

Lenin had felt it necessary to use the secret police (the Cheka) to prevent opposition to Bolshevik rule. Under Stalin, the secret police and prison camps (Gulags) were hugely expanded as Stalin started a campaign of mass arrests and executions known as 'the purges'. This period in history is often referred to as the 'Great Terror' and was triggered by the murder of the highly popular politician, Sergei Kirov.

THE MURDER OF KIROV

SOURCE A

Sergei Kirov (1886–1934).

On the afternoon of 1 December 1934, Kirov entered Leningrad party headquarters to continue a busy day of work. As well as being Party boss for this important city, he was a member of the Politburo. As Kirov made his way to his office, he did not seem to notice the absence of the usual NKVD guards. Waiting for him, however, was Leonid Nikolayev – a bitter, recently expelled Party member. Nikolayev drew his Nagant M1895 revolver, the standard issue side-arm for the army and police in Tsarist times, and shot Kirov in the back of the neck. Kirov died instantly.

Stalin immediately claimed that the assassination had been part of a plot led by Trotsky, Zinoviev and Kamenev to **overthrow** his government. Stalin argued that strong measures were needed to destroy this threat to the country. Within weeks of Kirov's death, the purges started. Thousands of Party members were arrested in Moscow and Leningrad, and shot. As the timeline shows, **Old Bolsheviks** were also arrested and accused of organising Kirov's murder.

▼ Timeline of the purges

January 1937 The second Moscow show trial; 17 'old Bolsheviks' are accused of Kirov's murder

August 1936
The first Moscow show trial. Zinoviev, Kamenev and 14 others are convicted of murdering Kirov

December 1934
Kirov is assassinated

June 1937
Tukhachevsky and leading army officers are shot

December 1938
Beria replaces Yezhov as head of the NKVD

February 1940
Yezhov is shot

February 1934
Kirov is widely cheered during the 17th Party Congress

January 1935
Zinoviev and Kamenev arrested for conspiracy to murder Kirov

September 1936
Yezhov becomes head of the NKVD (the People's Commissariat for Internal Affairs). A period of mass purges begins, known as the 'Great Terror'

May 1937
The purge of the Red Army begins

March 1938
The third Moscow show trial. Bukharin and 20 others are found guilty of killing Kirov

March 1939
Stalin declares an end to the mass purges at the 18th Party Congress

REMOVING POLITICAL OPPOSITION

Kirov's assassination in 1934 is one of the great murder mysteries of the Soviet Union. As Figure 3.1 shows, the events surrounding his death are highly suspicious. Historians have also found no evidence of any organised plot to overthrow the government. Instead, it is more likely that Kirov was killed on Stalin's orders. Although Stalin had won the power struggle, by the early 1930s, opposition to his rule was increasing.

- In the summer of 1932, Martemyan Ryutin, a senior member of the Party, bitterly attacked Stalin's policies of rapid industrialisation and collectivisation (see Source B). Because of this disloyalty, Stalin demanded his execution. Kirov and other members of the Politburo voted against Stalin, arguing successfully that killing fellow Party members was wrong. Instead, Ryutin was expelled from the Party and exiled.

▶ **Figure 3.1** The suspicious background to Kirov's assassination, suggesting it was planned by Stalin

SOURCE B

An extract from Ryutin's bitter criticism of Stalin in 1932.

[Stalin was] the evil genius of the Russian Revolution who, motivated by vindictiveness and lust for power, has brought the revolution to the edge of the abyss.

The gunman, Nikolayev, had twice been arrested near Kirov's office. The second time he was carrying a gun. Both times he was released.

Secret police officers responsible for investigating the murder were arrested and later shot.

Kirov's bodyguard was not with him when he was killed. The bodyguard later died in a traffic 'accident'.

Nikolayev was executed without standing trial.

- The 17th Party Congress of 1934 was designed to be a celebration of Stalin's economic policies. It was even called the Congress of Victors. While Stalin was widely applauded, so too was Kirov. People liked Kirov personally, but also approved of his call for more moderate policies.
- When the 17th Party Congress voted to approve the Central Committee, Kirov received more votes than Stalin, showing his popularity. Next, a group of old Party members tried to persuade Kirov to stand against Stalin for the position of General Secretary. Although Kirov refused, Stalin soon found out about the plan.

Stalin concluded that his position as leader was not completely secure. Organising the murder of Kirov was an ideal solution. Not only would it allow him to remove his main rival, but by blaming Kamenev and Zinoviev, Stalin could also get rid of his two old enemies from the power struggle. It also gave him an excuse to remove anyone in the wider party whose loyalty was doubted. This is why many people thought Stalin had arranged the murder himself.

TOTAL CONTROL

Stalin wanted to secure total control over the Communist Party, but he also believed there were other groups that needed to be disciplined. The purges gave him an ideal way of doing this.

- Instructions sent out from Moscow to local Communist Party organisations were often ignored. This became obvious in the dekulakisation drive, when many local Party workers proved unwilling to arrest kulaks because they knew them personally. By launching the purges and creating an atmosphere in which nobody felt safe, Stalin hoped that everyone would start following orders.

- The disruption caused by the Five Year Plans and collectivisation had created an unstable society. The new towns were dangerous, unruly places. People lived in overcrowded, unsanitary conditions. Arguments often broke out and became violent. Many of the ex-peasants forced to flee to the towns from the countryside felt a great anger towards the government. Stalin saw terror as a way of keeping these angry and unhappy people under control.

- Following Hitler's appointment as German Chancellor in 1933, war between Germany and the Soviet Union became increasingly likely. Hitler hated Communism and made no secret of his desire to invade the Soviet Union. To make the weapons of war under the third Five Year Plan, Stalin needed to drive his already exhausted and overworked labour force even harder. He also wanted to ensure that when war came, the Red Army would be completely loyal to him. Stalin believed that terror was the best way of achieving both aims.

STALIN'S PERSONALITY

KEY TERM

paranoid unreasonable belief that others are trying to harm you

The purges were partly driven by Stalin's **paranoid** personality. He was deeply distrustful and believed people would always betray him in the end. He saw threats and plots everywhere, even though they did not exist in reality. He held grudges for a long time and enjoyed taking revenge. He was also a rude man, and violence came easily to him.

These character faults became worse following the death of Stalin's wife, Nadya Alliluyeva, in 1932. She shot herself following an argument with Stalin – Nadya had expressed her horror at the Ukrainian famine and her husband had replied with vulgar abuse. At Nadya's funeral, Stalin said that 'she went away as an enemy'. Stalin felt betrayed but he also became more isolated. He mixed only with his close political circle, and spent most of his time either in his Kremlin office or his country house outside Moscow.

TERROR ECONOMICS

The purges were driven by economic need. The Gulags became a vital part of Stalin's industrialisation drive by providing a lot of slave labour. Prisoners were used to carry out dangerous work such as mining and logging in inhospitable regions. Many of the show-piece construction projects, such as the White Sea canal and Moscow metro, relied on forced labour. The purges made sure that this vital labour force was constantly available. By the end of the 1930s, the Gulag population stood at around 8 million.

KEY TERMS

scapegoat someone or something blamed even if they are innocent of the supposed wrong

wreckers a term to describe political opponents who deliberately attempted to damage the economy

The purges also gave Stalin a convenient **scapegoat** for the problems of the Five Year Plans, such as missed targets, low-quality output and high accident rates. Instead of focusing on the real causes, such as the faulty central planning process, he blamed '**wreckers**'. These 'enemies of the people' were deliberately sabotaging the economy on behalf of Trotsky, Zinoviev and Kamenev. Stalin even encouraged ordinary workers to report their factory managers and supervisors to the NKVD (see the table on page 48, 'The Soviet secret police and leadership') if the workers suspected their superiors of trying to block Stalin's reforms.

LENIN'S LEGACY

It is perhaps no surprise that Stalin started the purges. Terror had become a key part of the Communist system under Lenin.

■ Lenin had seized power in the October 1917 revolution, and soon after, he closed down the democratically elected **Constituent Assembly**.

■ Lenin had created the **repressive** Cheka and authorised the 'Red Terror' during the Civil War.

■ Lenin had shown his dislike of disagreement within the Party by creating the ban on factions in 1921.

Stalin also applied terror, but more ruthlessly and on a larger scale. Some historians have argued that Lenin's Red Terror was aimed at people he genuinely believed were opponents of the Bolsheviks. But Stalin was prepared to use exile to Siberia, imprisonment and execution against his opponents within the Party. This was an important difference between the approaches of the two leaders.

ACTIVITY

1 What do you think Ryutin meant in Source B?
2 Working in pairs, take turns in explaining the different causes of the purges to each other.

EXAM-STYLE QUESTION

A01   **A02**

SKILLS ▸ PROBLEM SOLVING, REASONING, DECISION MAKING, ADAPTIVE LEARNING, INNOVATION

'The main reason Stalin launched the purges was to remove his rivals in the Communist Party.' How far do you agree? Explain your answer.

You may use the following in your answer:
■ removing rivals
■ rapid industrialisation.
You **must** also use information of your own.   **(16 marks)**

HINT

To do well in this question, you need to give an overall judgement to the question. Do you think Stalin launched the purges mainly or only partly because of his wish to remove political rivals?

3.2 THE KEY FEATURES OF THE PURGES

LEARNING OBJECTIVES

☐ Understand the roles of Yezhov, the NKVD and the Gulags

☐ Understand why Stalin staged the Moscow Show Trials, as well as the key features of the trials

☐ Understand the impact of the purges.

THE ROLES OF YEZHOV, THE NKVD AND THE GULAG

To carry out the purges, Stalin used the Communist Party's secret police, known from 1934 as the NKVD. As the following table shows, this was the direct descendant of Lenin's blood-soaked Cheka. Its main purpose was to hunt out and destroy all threats to the Communist Party, which it did ruthlessly. NKVD officers spied on, intimidated and arrested people, forced confessions from those arrested, imposed sentences and carried these sentences out – nearly always either execution or 10 years' hard labour in the Gulag.

Nikolai Yezhov, head of the NKVD between 1936 and 1938.

EXTEND YOUR KNOWLEDGE

Yezhov was badly educated, starting his working life as a tailor's assistant and factory worker. He was a soldier in the Tsarist army during the First World War, but switched to the Bolsheviks just before the 1917 Russian Revolution. He rose quickly through the communist system, largely because of his cold efficiency and complete loyalty to Stalin. Because he was only five feet tall, many people called him the 'poison dwarf', as he was also a sadistic, nervous alcoholic, who personally supervised torture.

REASONS FOR AND FEATURES OF THE MOSCOW SHOW TRIALS, 1936–39

KEY TERM

show trial   a trial held in public, in which the outcome has already been decided

▼ The Soviet secret police and leadership

YEARS ACTIVE	SECRET POLICE	PEOPLE IN CHARGE
1917–22	Cheka (the All-Russian Commission to Fight Counter-Revolution, Sabotage and Speculation)	Felix Dzerzhinsky
1922–34	OGPU (the Department of Political Police)	Felix Dzerzhinsky Genrikh Yagoda
1934–43	NKVD (the People's Commissariat of Internal Affairs)	Genrikh Yagoda Nikolai Yezhov Lavrenti Beria

The Gulags were run by the NKVD. The following types of people could be found in Gulags by the end of the 1930s:
- common criminals
- workers and factory managers who had been convicted of wrecking
- Communist Party and government officials found guilty of plotting against the government
- foreign communists who had gone to live in the Soviet Union but were accused of spying
- artists, writers and university lecturers whose loyalty to Stalin was doubted
- leaders of **ethnic groups** who were seen as too independent by Stalin
- members of ethnic minority groups such as Poles and Koreans with links to bordering countries
- Red Army officers.

While some of the above were real opponents of the Soviet regime, most were completely innocent of any wrongdoing. This did not matter to Stalin; the Gulag's very existence helped terrify most of the population into obedience, and gave the Five Year Planners a plentiful supply of cheap labour.

From 1936 to 1938, the NKVD was headed by Nikolai Yezhov. A loyal Stalinist, he oversaw a dramatic increase in the number of victims of the purges by arresting members of the Communist Party, the Army and the general population. In the Soviet Union, this period became known as the *Yezhovschina* (Time of Yezhov) because no one was safe from arrest.

While most of the arrests, killings and deportations were not reported, three high-profile **show trials** were staged. In these, some of the greatest heroes of the 1917 Revolution and Civil War – the so-called Old Bolsheviks – confessed to plotting against the state. The charges were completely false and the evidence was made up, but for Stalin, the trials were very important:
- He wanted to remove once and for all his old rivals from the Party. The chief victims of the show trials were Kamenev, Zinoviev and Bukharin – his main opponents from the leadership struggle.
- Stalin wanted to frighten the wider Communist Party by showing them the results of not being loyal to him.
- He wanted to create a tense, paranoid atmosphere in the Soviet Union, in which people believed there were dangerous enemies, spies and wreckers at work.
- Stalin hoped people would unite behind him if they knew he was protecting them from dangerous enemies.

Following Kamenev and Zinoviev's executions, the bullets were dug out of their skulls, cleaned and then presented to Yagoda, head of the NKVD at the time. He labelled the bullets 'Zinoviev' and 'Kamenev', and kept them in his desk drawer, until his own arrest in 1937. Yagoda himself was tried in the third Moscow Show Trial alongside Bukharin, and executed.

SOURCE D

NKVD photograph of an exhausted Zinoviev, taken before his trial in 1936.

THE TRIAL OF THE SIXTEEN (1936)

The 'stars' of the first show trial were Zinoviev and Kamenev. They were charged with organising Kirov's murder, as well as plotting to disrupt the Five Year Plans and overthrow the government. Although they maintained their innocence in prison, both men **pleaded guilty** at the trial. The chief prosecutor, Andrey Vyshinsky, demanded that they 'Shoot the mad dogs', and the sentence was carried out the next day. While Kamenev met his death with dignity, Zinoviev, in despair and panic, begged for his life. For his amusement, Stalin later got his security chief to re-enact Zinoviev's last moments.

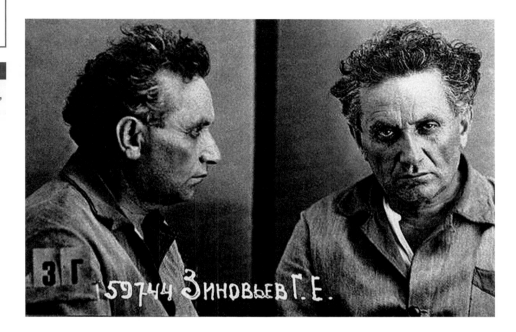

THE TRIAL OF THE SEVENTEEN (1937)

The second show trial focused on Trotsky's former allies. Charges once again included plotting to kill Kirov, overthrow the government and disrupt the Five Year Plans, and also maintaining contact with Trotsky. All pleaded guilty. Thirteen were executed, and the remaining four were sent to the Gulags, where they soon died.

THE TRIAL OF THE TWENTY-ONE (1938)

In the final show trial, Bukharin took centre stage. He was charged with attempting to overthrow the government, the murder of Kirov and, most amazingly, attempting to assassinate Lenin. During the trial, Bukharin did his best to highlight the ludicrous nature of the charges, but in the end he pleaded guilty. He was sentenced to death and Vyshinsky accused him of being 'a foul smelling heap of human garbage'. According to eyewitness reports, Bukharin died cursing Stalin.

Although he was living in exile in Mexico, Trotsky did not escape the purges. Stalin ordered the NKVD to kill him. Following a series of failed assassination attempts, an NKVD agent called Ramón Mercader entered Trotsky's study and slammed an ice pick into his head. Trotsky was taken to hospital in a coma and died the next day, aged 60. Mercader was sentenced to 20 years in prison for murder. He never revealed his NKVD connections, but was declared a Hero of the Soviet Union on his release.

The show trials were a **sham**, but why did the Old Bolsheviks confess? They were no doubt worn down by constant **interrogation** and **torture**. Deals were also made in return for full confessions. Stalin promised Kamenev and Zinoviev a full pardon, but he later broke his word. Bukharin agreed to confess in order to save his wife and young child. Just before his death, he wrote her a fond letter saying that one day his good name would be restored. He was right, but it would take until 1988.

Leon Trotsky was killed by an NKVD agent in August 1940.

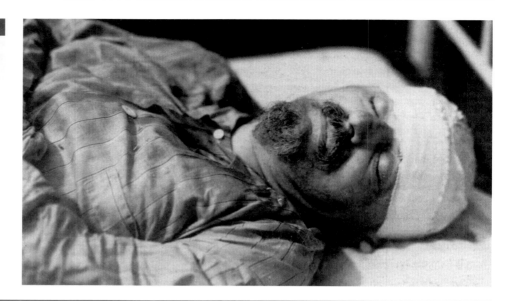

THE PURGE OF THE WIDER COMMUNIST PARTY

At the same time as the destruction of the Old Bolsheviks, the wider Party was purged. This is clearly shown by the fate of those who were Party members in 1934, right at the start of the purges.

- Altogether, 70 per cent of the 1934 Central Committee were later executed or imprisoned.
- Of the 1996 people who attended the 17th Party Congress of 1934, 1108 were later purged.
- Overall, it is estimated that 1 million Party members became victims of the purges.

EXTEND YOUR KNOWLEDGE

Much of the evidence used in the show trials was made up. For example, one of the defendants confessed to murdering Kirov at a time when he was already in prison. On another occasion, the court were told how the plotters met at the Hotel Bristol in Denmark – it later emerged the hotel had been demolished decades before, in 1917. Stalin, who received daily reports of the trials and sometimes attended, sitting hidden at the back of the court room, is reported to have shouted, 'What the devil did you need the hotel for? You ought to have said "railway station". The station is always there.'

PURGE OF THE ARMED FORCES

Having destroyed the independence of the Communist Party, Stalin's next target was the armed forces. He feared that its leaders would one day try to seize power from him for the following reasons.

- They were tough and independent minded.
- Having access to weapons and manpower, they had the means to remove Stalin.
- Many had been appointed by Trotsky and so Stalin did not fully trust them.

In May 1937, eight generals were arrested on charges of plotting with Germany and Japan to overthrow Stalin. They included the popular and talented Marshal Tukhachevsky. He was Chief of the General Staff, as well as one of the founders of the Red Army and a civil war hero. In reality, there was no plot. Tukhachevsky was an enthusiastic supporter of Stalin. However, following their brutal torture at the hands of the NKVD, all eight confessed to treason and were shot. Tukhachevsky's confession was even stained with his own blood.

In the following 18 months, the Soviet Union's military leadership was extensively purged.

■ The majority of the army's senior officers were shot, including three out of five marshals (the highest rank in the military) and 14 out of 16 army commanders.

■ Half of the army's junior officers – 35,000 men – were imprisoned or shot.

■ All the admirals of the Soviet navy were shot.

■ All except one of the senior commanders in the Soviet air force were shot.

CONTROL OF THE PEOPLE

SOURCE F

A description of the NKVD 'conveyor belt' method of interrogation by a victim of the purges.

Picture a group of about forty prisoners, men and women, all worn out, hungry, eaten by lice, suffering from swollen legs from long standing – people who have not slept for many nights. Single file we were led into a big room with three or four desks, and at each desk was an examining officer. Then comes another room and more examining officers, a corridor, stairs and more rooms with more examining officers. At the command 'at a run' we had to run from one desk to another. And as we approached each desk the examining officer would start shouting at us in the vilest language imaginable… This sort of torture lasts from ten to twelve hours. Examining officers go away and rest; they get tired sitting and shouting obscenities and so are relieved by others, but the prisoners have to keep on running.

SOURCE G

Nikolai Yezhov speaking to NKVD executioners.

There will be some innocent victims in this fight against Fascist agents. We are launching a major attack on the Enemy; let there be no resentment if we bump someone with an elbow. Better that ten innocent people should suffer than one spy get away. When you chop wood, chips fly.

Stalin signalled the need to widen the purges to ordinary people when, in July 1937, he called for the removal of all 'anti-Soviet elements' from society. Within a few weeks, Yezhov had made Operational Order 00447: a list of 250,000 people identified as 'enemies of the state', to be arrested by the end of that year. Following the target-driven approach of the Five Year Plans, each NKVD branch was given its own arrest quota to fulfil.

The NKVD was greatly helped by ordinary people. A mass media campaign was launched to encourage ordinary people to inform on their neighbours, work colleagues, friends and family. This resulted in a flood of **denunciations** – far more than the authorities ever expected. Some people used it as a way to settle old scores, to get a colleague's job, flat or possessions, or to move criticism away from themselves. In the paranoid atmosphere of the late 1930s, many people genuinely believed society was full of spies and **traitors**, and informed because they thought it was the right thing to do. As a result, a slip of the tongue or a careless act could result in arrest. For example:

■ An elderly tailor stuck his needle into a nearby newspaper before finishing work. He didn't notice that the needle went into the eye of a picture of a Communist Party official. A customer standing nearby informed the authorities, and within days, the tailor was sentenced to 10 years' hard labour.

■ A housewife was jailed because some pieces of soap she had purchased fell on to a newspaper picture of Joseph Stalin.

Most arrests came at night, between 11 p.m. and 3 a.m. NKVD officers drove in black vehicles nicknamed 'ravens' to collect their victims. The late-night knock at the door came to be deeply feared. Prisoners were then taken to the local NKVD prison and subjected to the 'conveyor belt' method of interrogation, described in Source F. This went on for several days and nights, and was often accompanied by extreme violence, as well as threats to arrest and execute members of the prisoner's family if they did not co-operate. In the end, most people signed the confession given to them, although the charges were usually completely false. They also gave the NKVD the names of 'accomplices', who in turn would be arrested.

In this way, the number of ordinary people caught up the purges rapidly increased. As Source G shows, the question of guilt or innocence did not matter to the NKVD. Fulfilling Stalin's wishes by meeting (or even exceeding) the arrest quotas was the most important thing.

After confession, a simple trial took place in front of three-man teams of NKVD officers (troikas). These almost always found the accused guilty. They then pronounced their sentence. Many victims were simply shot in the back of the head. There were even targets for this – the Politburo decided that 28 per cent of prisoners should be executed, with the rest being sentenced for up to 10 years' hard labour in the Gulags. Hundreds of mass graves have since been discovered. One of the largest was near the village of Butovo, a remote wooded area about 24 km south of Moscow. The victims were transported by night from central Moscow in food vans marked 'meat'. The awaiting executioners had free access to vodka and, afterwards, eau de cologne to remove the spell of blood and gunpowder. It is thought that during the late 1930s, more than 20,000 people were executed and buried at Butovo.

THE CONDITIONS IN THE GULAG

Those not shot were sent to the Gulag. As Figure 3.2 shows, this was an extensive system of forced labour camps, often located in some of the most inhospitable areas of the Soviet Union. It was a constant struggle just to survive in the camps.

SOURCE H

A typical Gulag workcamp.

- Typical Gulag labour was exhausting physical work – cutting down trees, mining coal, copper or gold, or building transport links and the new cities of the Five Year Plans. Only the most basic tools were provided.
- During non-working hours, prisoners lived in overcrowded, badly heated barracks, surrounded by a fence or barbed wire. They were watched by armed guards in watch towers.
- Random violence from guards was common.
- There was a divide between the two main types of inmates: professional criminals and political prisoners. The criminals received slightly better treatment from the guards and tended to bully the other prisoners.
- Prisoners received food according to how much work they did. A full ration provided just enough food for survival. Those who worked well could earn extra rations.
- Prisoners who failed to meet their daily work quotas had their rations cut. As a result, some prisoners slowly starved to death. They were referred to as 'goners' by the other inmates.

Kolyma, in the north-eastern corner of Siberia, was a name that struck fear into Gulag prisoners. The camps in this region were regarded as the toughest to survive. Kolyma was so remote that the journey took around 3 months.

▲ Figure 3.2 The Soviet Gulag system

Prisoners were transported in overcrowded and dirty trains across the length of the Soviet Union. They then boarded prison ships to take them to a remote wilderness. Prisoners spoke of Kolyma as a place where 12 months were winter and all the rest summer. Temperatures could fall to as low as -45 °C. The main purpose of the Kolyma camps was gold mining. Stalin needed this in order to buy machinery from the West. Other prisoners were building roads, railway lines, docks and the city of Magadan.

Gulag inmates constructing a railway in northern Siberia.

THE IMPACT OF THE PURGES

By the end of 1938, Stalin decided that the purges had gone far enough and he removed **Yezhov as head of the NKVD. The following** March, Stalin told the Party Congress that the purges were over. 'Undoubtedly,' said Stalin, 'we shall have no further need to resort to the methods of mass purges.' Stalin also joked about foreign suggestions that the trials of 'spies, assassins and wreckers' had weakened the Soviet state. He was wrong – the Soviet Union and its people had paid a terrible price.

EXTEND YOUR KNOWLEDGE

On 10 April 1939, Yezhov was secretly arrested and imprisoned. He broke quickly under torture and confessed to being an 'enemy of the people'. His trial began on 2 February 1940, during which he pleaded not guilty, claiming that his confession had been obtained under torture. He also said that he would die with the name of Stalin on his lips. When his death sentence was read out, Yezhov became hysterical and had to be dragged out of the room, struggling with the guards and screaming. Two days later, he was shot in the basement of a small NKVD station in Moscow. His body was immediately cremated and the ashes dumped in a common grave.

HUMAN COST

It is difficult to calculate exactly how many people were caught up in the purges. The evidence is full of gaps. Although the NKVD kept records, many of these were burnt as the Germans approached Moscow in 1941. A census was held in 1937, but its results were destroyed and the organisers sent to the Gulag, because it revealed a significant fall in the Soviet Union's population.

It is thought that the purges may have led to:
- 7–8 million arrests
- 1–1.5 million executions
- 7–8 million people sent to the Gulag
- 2 million deaths in the Gulag.

The impact of the purges was not spread evenly across society. Those most at risk were men aged 30–45 in management or professional positions. In addition, the NKVD had targets for different national groups. Manual workers and peasants were less likely to be arrested. Only 5 per cent of those arrested were women.

The climate of fear created by the purges meant that no one could feel safe. Normal human relationships broke down. To survive, it was easier to trust no one and avoid conversation – a careless comment could easily result in arrest. Anyone could be an informer, and countless numbers of ordinary people did inform on their neighbours and workmates.

WEAKENING OF THE SOVIET UNION

Officially, the purges were meant to strengthen the Soviet Union by removing wreckers, enemies of the people and spies. In fact, they had the opposite effect. Experienced members of the government including Gosplan officials, factory managers and highly trained scientists, engineers and workers were all targeted. The loss of their skills and experience damaged the economy and weakened the third Five Year Plan. This is highlighted by the performance of the Donbass region of Ukraine. It was of major importance to the Soviet economy, producing two-thirds of all coal. As the following table shows,

▼ Coal production in the Donbass region (millions of tonnes)

▽ YEAR	▽ PRODUCTION
1928	27
1932	45
1936	80
1940	82

performance in Donbass under the first two Five Year Plans was very strong, with a threefold increase in production between 1928 and 1936. However, in the late 1930s, more than one-quarter of mine managers were purged, causing production to level off.

ACTIVITY

Use the statistics in the table to decide how successful coal production was under each of the three Five Year Plans.

The removal of 35,000 officers damaged the quality of leadership in the Red Army. The impact of this was felt when the Soviet Union went to war against Finland in 1939–40 in order to push Finland's borders away from Leningrad. Expecting a quick victory over a much smaller force, the Red Army instead suffered 200,000 casualties and was fought to a complete stop. Similarly, a lack of experienced officers contributed to military failure when the Germans invaded in 1941.

POLITICAL IMPACT

For Stalin, the purges had achieved one important result. He was now the unchallenged leader of the Soviet Union. Every potential threat had been crushed, including:
- the Old Bolsheviks, who had once opposed Stalin
- the wider Communist Party, who one day might have thrown their support behind another leader
- the military, which was the only organisation with the power to remove Stalin
- the ordinary people, whose general discontent could have developed into something more threatening.

SOURCE J

Stalin reportedly told the following joke about a delegation from Georgia.

They come, they talk to Stalin, and then they go, heading off down the Kremlin's corridors. Stalin starts looking for his pipe. He can't find it. He calls in Beria, the dreaded head of his secret police.

'Go after the delegation, and find out which one took my pipe,' he says.

Beria scuttles off down the corridor.

Five minutes later, Stalin finds his pipe under a pile of papers. He calls Beria:

'Look, I've found my pipe.'

'It's too late,' Beria says. 'Half the delegation admitted they took your pipe, and the other half died during questioning.'

ACTIVITY

What does Source J reveal about the Soviet Union under Stalin?

EXAM-STYLE QUESTION

A01   **A02**

Explain **two** effects on the Soviet Union of Stalin's purges.   **(8 marks)**

HINT

Remember to give two effects. The maximum mark for explaining one effect is four.

3.3 PROPAGANDA

LEARNING OBJECTIVES

☐ Understand the meaning of the terms 'propaganda' and 'censorship', as well as their importance to Stalin's dictatorship

☐ Understand the reasons for and the key features of Stalin's cult of personality

☐ Understand how the Soviet Union's cultural life was impacted by socialist realism.

Despite the scale of the purges, ordinary people did not obey Stalin out of fear alone. This is because along with terror, the Soviet government used propaganda to build up a genuine level of support for the Soviet dictator.

▶ **Figure 3.3** The key features of Soviet propaganda

KEY POINT

It is important you understand the difference between propaganda and censorship. Propaganda is using information to create the message you want. Censorship is blocking information in case it creates the message you don't want!

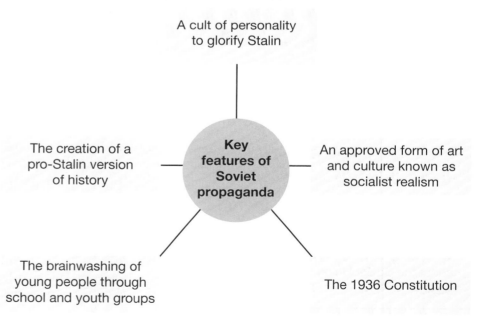

A cult of personality to glorify Stalin

The creation of a pro-Stalin version of history

Key features of Soviet propaganda

An approved form of art and culture known as socialist realism

The brainwashing of young people through school and youth groups

The 1936 Constitution

THE METHODS OF THE CULT OF PERSONALITY

The most striking feature of Soviet propaganda was Stalin's **cult of personality**. The Soviet leader was built into a god-like figure. He was referred to as the *Vozhd*, or 'the big hero', and as Extract A shows, his image was everywhere. Adoration of Stalin was constant. Journalists, artist, writers and poets tried to outdo each other in describing his incredible qualities.

KEY TERM

cult of personality where people are encouraged to admire and praise a well-known person

School and youth groups taught children to love Stalin more than their parents. When his name was mentioned, people leapt to their feet with sudden applause. The cult of personality stressed the following main themes.

EXTRACT A

An American novelist describes visiting the Soviet Union in 1947.

Everything in the Soviet Union takes place under the fixed stare of the plaster, bronze, drawn or embroidered eye of Stalin. His portrait does not just hang in every museum but in a museum's every room. Statues of him dignify the facade of every public building. His bust stands in front of all airports, railway station and bus stations. A bust of Stalin stands in every classroom. In shops they sell million upon million of images of him, and in every home there is at least one portrait of him.

EXAM-STYLE QUESTION

AO4

SKILLS ANALYSIS, INTERPRETATION, CREATIVITY

Study Extract A. What impression does the author give about Soviet propaganda? You must use Extract A to explain your answer. **(6 marks)**

HINT

To do well in this question, you need to identify one overall impression and explain how the extract shows this. In this case, for example, it could be that Soviet propaganda was everywhere.

STALIN AS POLITICAL GENIUS

Stalin was shown as Lenin's right-hand man in the early days of Communist rule and then Lenin's natural successor. Slogans such as 'Stalin is the Lenin of today' were everywhere, and propaganda claimed that he was the one person capable of guiding the Soviet Union to its Communist future. In reality, Stalin was not a great political thinker and never enjoyed the close relationship with Lenin claimed by Soviet propaganda.

SOURCE K

A 1938 painting showing Lenin and Stalin together.

ACTIVITY

Study Source K. How does it subtly suggest that Stalin was in fact more important than Lenin?

STALIN AS THE GREAT ECONOMIC PLANNER

He was seen as responsible for all the 'successes' of the Five Year Plans. Posters featured him looking out over landscapes of busy factories, highly mechanised collective farms and showpiece projects like the Dnieper Dam. As Source L shows, poets heaped praise on Stalin. The obvious failures of the economy were either blamed on 'wreckers' or not mentioned.

SOURCE L

This extract is taken from a speech to the 17th Congress of Soviets in February 1935 by a Soviet writer.

Centuries will pass, and the generations still to come will regard us as the happiest of mortals, as the most fortunate of men, because we lived in the century of centuries, because we were privileged to see Stalin, our inspired leader. Yes, and we regard ourselves as the happiest of mortals because we are the contemporaries of a man who never had an equal in world history. The men of all ages will call on your name, which is strong, beautiful, wise and marvellous. Your name is engraved on every factory, every machine, every place on the earth, and in the hearts of all men.

SOURCE M

Six-year-old Engelsina Cheshkova embraces Stalin. Propaganda pictures like these were often accompanied by the slogan 'Thank you comrade Stalin for my happy childhood'.

STALIN AS THE MAN OF THE PEOPLE

In the 1930s, Stalin was normally shown wearing plain clothes, smoking a pipe and walking alongside ordinary workers and peasants. To develop a fatherly image, he was often pictured with adoring children. Stalin's tiny childhood home in Gori, Georgia was even turned into a place of worship. This helped draw attention to his humble origins. In reality, Stalin rarely mixed with ordinary people. He even had the parents of Engelsina Cheshkova, featured in Source M, sent to the Gulag.

STALIN AS GENERALISSIMO

After the Second World War, Stalin was shown as the great war leader who had independently planned and led the Soviet victory over Nazi Germany. He was often pictured in a striking white military uniform. His costly military mistakes and the leading role played by his generals were ignored.

THE REASONS FOR THE CULT OF PERSONALITY

Publicly, Stalin always said that Lenin, the Soviet Union and its people were more important than him, but he did nothing to discourage the cult of personality. This is because it brought him a range of political benefits.

1 Stalin used it to increase his own power over the Communist party. The cult of personality increased his reputation and dramatically placed him ahead of the country's other leading politicians. As long as Stalin was viewed as a near-god, no one could hope to challenge him.

2 Showing Stalin as a genius and as Lenin's natural successor gave his rule a sense of legitimacy. He was leading the Soviet Union because he was by far the best man for the job.

3 The impact of rapid industrialisation and collectivisation meant that the 1930s were a confusing time for many. The cult of personality gave reassurance and comfort. Ordinary people could put their trust in Stalin, believing he would lead them to a better life.

4 By encouraging absolute loyalty to one person, the Soviet Union was given a sense of unity. This tactic had a long tradition. In Tsarist times, the Russian people were brought together around a shared love of the royal family. Given the strains caused by mass industrialisation and collectivisation, this need to bring the nation together was particularly important.

5 The cult of personality allowed people to complain about everyday difficulties without ever criticising Stalin. As most people could not imagine that Stalin would be responsible, they directed their anger towards lower-level officials. 'If only Stalin knew, he would sort it out' was a popular saying, even in the time of the Great Terror.

SOCIALIST REALISM

After coming to power in 1917, the Communists encouraged artists, writers, musicians and film-makers to experiment with new forms of creativity. This helped to make the Soviet Union a leading centre of the arts in the 1920s. Stalin ended this creative freedom. He wanted art and culture to spread simple, direct communist propaganda to the ordinary people. As a result, the cultural life of the Soviet Union was brought under strict government control. A new artistic style, which had to be followed, was introduced. It was called socialist realism, and Figure 3.4 outlines some of its main rules.

▶ Figure 3.4 Checklist for socialist realism

Communist Party

Will the poorly educated masses be able to understand your work? ☐

Does it involve everyday situations? Factories, mines, collective farms, schools are all good. ☐

Family and home settings are not allowed. ☐

Does it show an ideal version of life under Communism? Do not show the grim reality. ☐

Are ordinary people shown as heroes? ☐

Is the act of everyday work made to feel important and noble? ☐

Will it inspire people about Stalin and the Communist project? ☐

ART

Source N shows a typical painting in the socialist realist style. It was an idealised image of life, which showed a land of plenty and celebrated ordinary people and their contribution to building communism.

SOURCE N

A painting from 1930 called *The Teenagers. The Laugh.*

MUSIC AND DANCE

Music had to be happy and positive. Folk songs were preferred. Pieces of classical music had to be in the major key, as this was considered a more pleasing sound. Jazz music was dismissed as immoral. Socialist realism extended even to dance. Complex, experimental dance could not be performed because it was difficult to understand. Traditional ballet dancing, which could be appreciated easily, was encouraged.

LITERATURE

The standard plot of socialist realist novels involved a peasant or worker hero being guided to even greater things by the Communist Party. So that they could be read by the newly literate population, novels had to have simple, direct language. One of the most popular novels was *How the Steel was Tempered* by Nikolai Ostrovsky (1936). It told the story of a young revolutionary named Pavel Korchagin and his heroic role in the Civil War. Although badly wounded and in great pain, after the war he put all of his efforts into rebuilding the country. Another widely read novel was *Cement* by Fyodor Gladkov (1925). Its hero, Gleb Chumalov, helped by a group of dedicated workers, brought a cement factory back into production after the Civil War, despite countless problems.

ACTIVITY

Are you surprised that two very popular novels in the Soviet Union at this time were about steel and cement? Explain your answer.

SOURCE O

The 24-metre-high, stainless steel statue called *Worker and Kolkhoz Woman*.

As Source O shows, sculpture, like art, focused on the ordinary people building communism and attempted to show them as heroes.

CINEMA

Films were used to retell epic events in Soviet and Russian history. One of the most popular was *Chapaev* (1934), directed by the Vasilyev brothers. It was based on the true life story of Chapaev, who rose from his peasant background to become a Civil War hero, before dying in a White attack in 1919. Another high-profile film was *Alexander Nevsky* (1938) by Sergei Eisenstein. It told how a great leader, Prince Alexander, helped by the common people, was able to defeat an invasion by knights from Germany in the 13th century.

ACTIVITY

1 In small groups, take on the role of ambitious young film-makers living in the Soviet Union in the 1930s. Develop an outline for a new film including a plot, important characters and the film's key message. Remember to think of a working title for your film, and make sure it follows the rules of socialist realism.

2 Next, team up with another group. The first group should 'pitch' (try to sell) their film idea. The second group should take on the role of Communist Party officials and decide, with reasons, whether or not the film should be given approval to be made.

THE NEW SOVIET CONSTITUTION OF 1936

In 1936, just as the mass arrests were beginning, Stalin created a new **constitution** for the Soviet Union. He even encouraged ordinary citizens to organise meetings and discuss its democratic terms, as outlined in Figure 3.5.

The Constitution was pure propaganda and the rights it guaranteed were not real. Only Communist Party candidates were allowed to enter elections, and only approved newspapers and magazines could be published. The right to a fair trial and other important rights could be, and were, ignored 'in the interest of national security'.

So why did Stalin do it?

■ Stalin was attempting to appeal to ordinary Soviet citizens. It made him look like a leader who cared about them.

■ He was trying to improve the poor image of the Soviet Union abroad. This was important because he wanted to work with the democratic countries in the West in order to stop the rise of Nazi Germany.

ACTIVITY

Based on what you have learned in this chapter, write a speech to present to a small group on what you think it was like to live in the Soviet Union under Stalin.

Direct elections of government	Housing
A job	Education
End of discrimination against 'class enemies'	Freedom of religion
Leisure	Freedom of the press and the right to meet
Paid holidays	Protection for individuals and their homes from interference and mistreatment
Health care	
Right to vote from age 18	
Secret ballot	

◀ **Figure 3.5** Rights promised in the 1936 Constitution

CENSORSHIP

KEY TERM

censorship the suppression of ideas or information

Information was tightly controlled in the Soviet Union. Along with propaganda putting out the official Soviet view of events, there was also a strict **censorship** system. Government censors prevented the publication of anything that contained critical opinions of the government or the wrong political message. They carefully checked the content of newspapers, radio broadcasts, films, books, posters, paintings, plays, ballet and music. As a result of the government's power to remove information or opinions that it did not like, it was in an extremely powerful position. It was able to restrict public debate by censoring any topics that it did not wish to be discussed.

Creative life suffered as a result of censorship. Any art form not meeting the standards of socialist realism was banned. In 1936, for example, 30 films and 10 plays were taken out of print for containing the wrong political message. One of these was the opera *Lady Macbeth of Mtsensk*, by the internationally known composer Shostakovich. It was accused of being too '**bourgeois**' – Stalin did not like the style of the music or the singing, and he was offended by one passionate scene involving Lady Macbeth.

The few individuals who tried to keep their artistic freedom faced severe consequences. In 1933, the poet Osip Mandelstam made up a poem about Stalin called 'The Kremlin Mountaineer' (Source P). Although he never wrote it down, he performed it to a small group of friends – one turned out to be an NKVD informer. Mandelstam was arrested and later died in a labour camp. As he said, 'Only in Russia is poetry respected, it gets people killed.'

SOURCE P

'The Kremlin Mountaineer', by Osip Mandelstam.

We live, deaf to the land beneath us,
Ten steps away no one hears our speeches,

But where there's so much as half a conversation
The Kremlin's mountaineer will get his mention.

His fingers are fat as grubs
And the words, final as lead weights, fall from his lips,

His cockroach whiskers leer
And his boot tops gleam.

Around him a rabble of thin-necked leaders –
fawning half-men for him to play with.

They whinny, purr or whine
As he prates and points a finger,

One by one forging his laws, to be flung
Like horseshoes at the head, the eye or the groin.

And every killing is a treat
For the broad-chested Ossete.

ACTIVITY

In small groups, discuss the different ways Mandelstam attacked Stalin in this poem.

So how did ordinary people respond to the constant flow of pro-government news stories, art and culture? Most simply accepted what they read and saw. Those who were not convinced had to turn to rumours, gossip or jokes such as Source Q to find out the truth. There was no other source of reliable information.

SOURCE Q

A Soviet joke told during the time of the Great Terror.

Question: 'Why do Soviet doctors remove tonsils through the backside?'

Answer: 'Because nobody dares open their mouth.'

EXTEND YOUR KNOWLEDGE

Totalitarianism is a political system in which ordinary people have no power and are completely controlled by the government. It aims to maintain total control over every aspect of society, including the public and private lives of its citizens. This label has been applied to regimes including Stalin's Soviet Union and Hitler's Germany.

3.4 CONTROL OF EDUCATION AND THE SOVIET INTERPRETATION OF HISTORY

LEARNING OBJECTIVES

☐ Understand why the young were especially targeted with propaganda

☐ Understand how the Communist Party controlled education and youth groups

☐ Understand how history was changed to benefit Stalin.

The Communist regime was particularly keen on targeting young people with propaganda. Their views were easier to shape than those of adults. As you will see more fully in Chapter 4, the education system was reformed during the 1930s so that it stressed total obedience to Stalin and the Communist Party. As a result, the more informal approach of the 1920s was replaced with strict classroom discipline, compulsory uniforms, examinations and a national curriculum supported by government-written textbooks. These were full of propaganda, as the teaching of history highlights.

There was one official version of history, approved by Stalin and taught to all school children. To help build pride in their country, children learned inspiring tales of the great Russian leaders of the past such as Ivan the Terrible, Peter the Great and Lenin. The climax of the story was, however, Stalin. In 1938, he ordered the writing of two new history books which had to be used in schools:
■ *The Short Course of the History of the All Union Communist Party*
■ *The Short Biography of Stalin*.

These wrongly showed Stalin as the main organiser of the 1917 revolution with Lenin, as well as showing him as a hero of the Civil War. Trotsky's leading role was completely ignored. As Sources R and S show, to support this rewriting of history, photographs were changed.

The original photo of Lenin addressing troops in Moscow, 1920, with Trotsky and Kamenev standing to the right of the platform.

In the 1930s, this became the standard version of the image. Trotsky and Kamenev had been airbrushed out of history.

Outside of school, children were expected to join youth organisations – the Pioneers for those under 14, and Komsomol for those aged 14–28. Although not officially compulsory, the Komsomol had over 10 million members by 1940. Children promised loyalty to Stalin and were taught how to be good communists. To guide them, the authorities held Pavlik Morozov up as a role model. He was a 14-year-old boy from the Urals who had denounced his own father to the authorities for helping kulaks. Later, Morozov was murdered by members of his own family in revenge. The government turned Morozov into a hero and erected statues in his honour. The message was clear: loyalty to Stalin was more important than family ties.

RECAP

RECALL QUESTIONS

1 Which politician was murdered in 1934, triggering the purges?
2 From 1934, what was the Soviet secret police called?
3 Which two well-known politicians confessed to plotting against the state in the first Moscow show trial, 1936?
4 How many junior officers were purged from the Red Army?
5 What was the population of the Gulag camps by the late 1930s?
6 Where were the most feared Gulag camps located?
7 What name was given to Stalin, meaning 'great hero'?
8 What was the name of the official style that all artists and writers had to follow under Stalin?
9 Which play did Stalin ban because he believed it contained the wrong political messages?
10 Who was murdered by his own family for denouncing his own father to the authorities?

CHECKPOINT

STRENGTHEN
S1 Describe the three Moscow show trials in not more than 50 words.
S2 Outline four important features of life in the Gulag.
S3 What is 'censorship'? How is it different to propaganda?

CHALLENGE
C1 'Far from being a powerful leader, the purges showed Stalin to be weak and insecure.' How far do you agree with this view?
C2 Why do you think Stalin's government made such an effort to encourage the cult of Stalin?
C3 'Soviet propaganda had little to do with the truth.' How far do you agree with this statement? Explain your answer fully.

SUMMARY

■ Following the murder of Kirov, Stalin claimed the purges were necessary to destroy a plot aimed at overthrowing the Communist government, but this was a lie.
■ In reality, Stalin launched the purges mainly to bring the Party, army and country under his complete control.
■ The purges were carried out by Stalin's secret police, known as the NKVD and led by Yezhov.
■ In a series of show trials, Zinoviev, Kamenev and Bukharin all confessed to plotting against the government, but the confessions were false and the evidence made up.
■ Huge numbers of innocent people were killed by the NKVD, or imprisoned in the Gulag camp system.
■ As well as using terror, Stalin employed propaganda and censorship as another means of controlling the population.
■ Stalin's cult of personality is an example of propaganda. He was portrayed as a near-god. History was rewritten to make him seem more important.
■ Art and culture had to follow the rules of socialist realism and show an idealised version of life, rather than the reality.
■ Young people were subject to propaganda both in school and through the Communist youth organisation, known as the Komsomol.

EXAM GUIDANCE: PART (C) QUESTIONS

A01 **A02**

SKILLS PROBLEM SOLVING, REASONING, DECISION MAKING, ADAPTIVE LEARNING, INNOVATION

Question to be answered: 'The main impact of Stalin's purges of the 1930s was the removal of opposition to Stalin.' How far do you agree? Explain your answer.

You may use the following in your answer:
- removal of opposition
- weakening the Soviet army.

You **must** also use information of your own. (16 marks)

Analysis Question: What do I have to do to answer the question well?

- You have been given two topics on which to write: the removal of opposition and the weakening of the Soviet army. You don't have to use the stimulus material provided and can use other factors. However, you will find it hard to assess the removal of opposition if you don't write about it!

- You must avoid just giving the information. You have to explain how the purges led to each impact.

- You are also asked to consider whether the removal of opposition was the **main** impact, so you will need to compare the effects.

- You have been given the weakening of the Soviet army as another reason, but you will see that the question says you must use information of your own. So you should include at least one impact other than those you have been given.

- That impact might be on ordinary people or the Soviet economy. If you include one of those, then you have three impacts to explain.

- In summary, to score very high marks on this question, you need to give:
  - coverage of content range (at least three factors)
  - coverage of arguments for and against the statement
  - clear reasons (criteria) for an overall judgement, backed by a convincing argument.

This is a very well-explained paragraph, directly focused on the question. You explain why political opposition was a concern for Stalin and how the purges silenced this.

Answer

I mainly agree that the main impact of the purges was the removal of opposition to Stalin. Although Stalin had won the power struggle, opposition to him was mounting by the mid-1930s. This was because collectivisation had led to famine in Ukraine. The first Five Year Plan had also caused a sharp fall in living standards. A senior Party official called Ryutin even spoke out against Stalin. Some in the Party were looking to Kirov as a possible replacement to Stalin. Stalin knew this and used the purges to kill or imprison any potential opponents. Kirov was murdered, and Stalin was most likely responsible. All Stalin's opponents from the leadership struggle including Zinoviev and Bukharin were placed on trial, found guilty and shot. In total over 1 million party members were killed or imprisoned. As a result, by the end of the 1930s no one in the Party dared speak out against Stalin. The purges therefore increased Stalin's power by removing all opposition.

Good. You use the first sentence to link to the question and indicate the weight you are giving to this factor. The level of historical knowledge is excellent.

Although not the main impact, the weakening of the Soviet army was also important. From 1937 to 1939 many of the leaders of the Red Army were shot or imprisoned. This included three out of five marshals, who were the highest-ranked leaders in the army, as well as 35,000 junior army officers. The loss of these leaders weakened the army. This was made clear in 1940 when the Red Army invaded the tiny nation of Finland. It should have been an easy fight, but it cost the Soviets 200,000 casualties. When Germany invaded in 1941, Stalin released many of the officers who had been placed in prison camps in order to try to undo some of the damage the purges had done. The impact of the purges on the army was therefore significant.

The economic impact of the purges is a good choice for an additional impact, beyond the two stimulus points. You have explained how the purges damaged the economy and have given evidence to prove this.

Finally, the purges damaged the Soviet economy. Stalin wanted to build as many factories as quickly as possible. This is why he launched three Five Year Plans during the 1930s. However, during the purges, workers were encouraged to inform on their factory bosses and skilled engineers if they did not think they were doing a good enough job. As a result of this, many people who were important to the economy were arrested. This damaged the third Five Year Plan in particular. Coal production in the Donbass region, for example, rapidly increased up to 1936. However, when the purges hit, many skilled workers were arrested and between 1936 and 1940 coal production hardly increased at all. This mattered because Donbass was the Soviet Union's main coal area. As a result the purges harmed the Soviet economy.

Your conclusion attempts to answer the question directly by considering the 'how far' aspect. All three impacts are mentioned in the conclusion, but you have restated your earlier points, rather than comparing the importance. You need to say how one factor was more important than the others.

I therefore mainly agree that the main impact of the purges was to remove opposition to Stalin. There had been mounting criticism in the Party and the purges silenced it all. However, there were other impacts. The Red Army was damaged as many of its leaders were killed. The economy was also damaged for the same reason. Overall the purges did not benefit the Soviet Union at all, only Stalin.

What are the strengths and weaknesses of this answer?
This is a very good answer. It explains three impacts of the purges and finishes with a well-reasoned conclusion. But to get the very highest mark, your comparison needs to compare the impacts, rather than treating them separately.

Answer checklist
☐ Identifies causes
☐ Provides detailed information to support the causes
☐ Shows how the causes led to the given outcome
☐ Provides a factor other than those given in the question
☐ Addresses 'main reason' by looking at arguments for and against, and comparing.

4. LIFE IN THE SOVIET UNION, 1924–41

LEARNING OBJECTIVES

☐ Understand the effects of Stalin's policies on living and working conditions in the towns and countryside

☐ Understand the differing experiences of social groups; changes in education and family life

☐ Understand the reasons for, and features of, the persecution of ethnic minorities.

When the Bolsheviks had seized power in 1917, they imagined building a communist society without poverty or hard labour. It would be a land of plenty where everyone's needs would be met. Machines would do the hard work, giving people the freedom to carry out jobs that genuinely interested them. Along with fulfilling and meaningful work, more time could be devoted to recreation and self-improvement. The Bolsheviks believed that society would no longer be spoiled by ugly divisions. The previous political system had allowed the rich to exploit the poor, men to control women and nations to dominate other nations. In a communist future, everyone would be equal.

Soon after the revolution, steps were taken to establish this brave new world. Efforts were made to improve the lives of women and ethnic minorities, two groups who had been repressed by the Tsarist regime. In the spirit of experimentation, schooling was radically reformed. However, these progressive trends were largely reversed by Stalin in the 1930s. Meanwhile, living and working conditions were sacrificed for the needs of rapid industrialisation. By 1941, therefore, the Communist land of plenty and equality still seemed a distant dream.

4.1 EFFECTS OF STALIN'S POLICIES ON LIVING AND WORKING CONDITIONS IN TOWN AND COUNTRYSIDE

LEARNING OBJECTIVES

- Understand the poor living conditions in town and countryside
- Understand the difficult working conditions for workers and peasants
- Understand some of the measures taken by the Communist government to improve daily life.

In 1935, Stalin announced that 'life has become better, comrades, life has become more joyous'. If he truly believed this, then he did not know his country. Stalin's polices of forced industrialisation and collectivisation led to an overall decline in working and living conditions for most Soviet citizens.

LIVING CONDITIONS IN TOWNS

Housing was a major issue for Soviet workers. Stalin's policy of rapid industrialisation caused an explosion in the size of the Soviet Union's towns and cities.

- Moscow's population increased from 2.2 million in 1929 to 4.1 million in 1936.
- Leningrad's population increased from 1.6 million in 1926 to 3.4 million in 1939.

The state was not prepared to spend its limited resources on building new housing. Instead, it simply divided up the already small apartments. The average family apartment declined from 5.5 square metres in 1930 to just 4 square metres in 1940. Many families ended up living in a single room, with a communal kitchen and bathroom. And those families were the lucky ones. Those waiting to receive a flat were the so-called 'corner dwellers' – home could be a coal shed, an under-stair cupboard, corridor or communal kitchen.

EXTEND YOUR KNOWLEDGE

The lack of investment in living conditions meant that in one Moscow district, there was not a single bathhouse between 650,000 people. Things were slightly better in Magnitogorsk. By 1939, there were enough public baths to allow each person seven baths per year.

ACTIVITY

1 Working in groups, measure out 4 square metres, the size of a typical Russian apartment in 1940.
2 Try to imagine how you would arrange all your most important possessions in this space.
3 Discuss the practicalities of how a typical Russian family of two adults and two children could exist in this area. What problems and issues would arise from living in such cramped conditions?

HOUSING IN NEW TOWNS

Lack of adequate housing was even more of an issue in the new factory towns which were constructed under the Five Year Plans. Magnitogorsk's population went from 25 people in 1929 to 250,000 in 1932. Like many of the new towns, the workers were initially housed in tents or mud huts. Although housing conditions slowly improved throughout the 1930s, they were still basic, and were mainly barrack-style dormitories.

SOURCE A

Early tent accommodation for workers at Magnitogorsk.

KEY TERM

wild-west town a quickly built and lawless town common in the mid west of the USA in the 19th century

In new towns like Magnitogorsk, workers also had to cope with unpaved roads which turned to mud in winter, no street lighting, open sewers and a lack of public transport. Magnitogorsk in the early 1930s had the feel of a **wild-west town**. Crime and violence were common, and it was dangerous to go out at night, especially for women.

EVERYDAY ITEMS

In the 1930s, it wasn't just bad housing that was a problem; daily life was also tough for the average worker. The Five Year Plans focused on developing heavy industry. Useful everyday items for people were not a priority. As a result, many basic items – such as shoes and clothing – were in short supply. Queues were sometimes longer than 1,000 people when shoes were available. More luxurious items, such as watches and furniture, were even harder to find. For many, stealing supplies from work became the normal way to get by. One popular proverb from the time stated that 'he who does not steal, robs his family'.

Similarly, the problems caused by collectivisation meant there was not enough food. Bread was rationed until 1935, for example. Even after this, shortages were common. The diet of the average worker was well below that of an average worker in 1900. In order to get the small supplies, queuing for food became a normal part of everyday life. Some people started waiting outside food shops at two in the morning, even in winter, when temperatures were well below freezing.

LEISURE OPPORTUNITIES

The authorities were well aware of how difficult everyday life was. Working with an extremely limited budget, they did try to develop leisure opportunities. Gorky Park, built in 1928, became a favourite destination for Muscovites (people from Moscow), for example. It offered attractive gardens, snack bars, a swimming pool, and a music and dance area where, in the summer evenings, couples danced to the latest tunes.

Many other towns also had parks, football stadiums, athletics grounds and cinemas. The cinema in Magnitogorsk soon had annual audiences of 600,000. These high figures show that although many of the films contained strong political messages, the audiences clearly enjoyed them. Exciting Civil War films were especially popular, and were the Russian equivalent to the Hollywood 'Western'. Another favourite activity for a Magnitogorsk resident was the 'mini' Olympics, held between teams from the various factories. Success meant the opportunity to compete against other factories at a regional level.

LIVING CONDITIONS IN THE COUNTRYSIDE

Compared to the towns, life was even harder in the countryside.
- Peasants did not get as much to eat as town workers, because they were regarded as less important. Some farm workers had to travel to town to buy bread, as there was so little food available on the farms.
- Peasants had always lived in very basic housing, typically a one-room wooden hut, with an outside toilet and water taken from the well (a deep hole in the ground). Collectivisation did not change this.
- The villages received very little new investment and so had none of the new leisure opportunities that town workers did.

WORKING CONDITIONS IN TOWNS

Whether digging in a mine, building a new factory or making steel, industrial work involved hard, physical effort. The Communist regime, which aimed to industrialise as rapidly as possible, was not focused on trying to improve already tough jobs. As a result, working conditions under the Five Year Plans became increasingly difficult.
- Health and safety was not a priority. As Source B shows, accidents at work were common. Meeting targets was more important to Stalin than safe workplaces.
- Internal passports, with their recognisable green covers, were introduced to try to stop workers constantly changing jobs in search of better employment. Police could ask to see a person's internal passport at any time. If the worker didn't have the 'right' to be in that city or workplace, they could be arrested and imprisoned.
- The rights of trade unions were severely restricted. Managers were given the power to sack workers and set wages without the need to gain the approval of the trade unions.
- 'Progressive piecework' was introduced. Workers no longer had a set wage, but were paid by the amount they produced. This was a move away from the Party's earlier belief in equal wages for workers. It also meant people had to work even harder for better pay.
- By the late 1930s, war with Nazi Germany was looking increasingly likely. The third Five Year Plan made the armaments industries a priority, and the state required even more effort from its workers. As Figure 4.1 shows, the 1940 Labour Code set out unpleasant regulations.

SOURCE B

A female worker describes her working day at the Dnieper Hydroelectric Power Station.

We were working on Section 34. I was sending up concrete, 95 tubs that day. We raised the tub. Suddenly I saw some tar paper fall into it. I went to get it, then started back. The board under me began to sink, and I was dragged down. I grabbed hold of the ladder, but my hand was slipping. Everybody got scared, one of the girls screamed. Another ran over to me, grabbed hold of my hand and dragged me out. I was full of concrete... the tar singed my arms. I went to dry off and then straight back to work.

▶ **Figure 4.1** The 1940 Labour Code

- **The working day will be increased from 7 to 8 hours.**

- **The working week will be lengthened from 5 out of 6 to 6 out of 7 days.**

- **Changing jobs without official permission will now be a criminal offence.**

- **If you are late to work by just 20 minutes on two occasions, your pay will be cut by 25 per cent for 6 months.**

EXTEND YOUR KNOWLEDGE

Real wages (what wages could buy) fell by over half during the first Five Year Plan, and were still well below their 1928 level in 1940.

SOURCE C

Two Russian workers eating black bread and soup at a table in front of a wall covered with Soviet Communist Workers posters.

Although the Five Year Plans did see a decline in working conditions, there were some positives. Everyone had a job. With unemployment levels in the early 1930s reaching 25 per cent of the workforce in some Western countries as a result of the Great Depression, this achievement must not be underestimated. Factories also gave basic clothing to their workers and set up canteens which made cheap, hot meals. Larger factories also set up childcare centres and laundry facilities. This eased the burden on women, who still had to carry out the majority of domestic tasks. Finally, rewards including pay or ration increases were available to those classed as shock workers, or better still, Stakhanovites.

SOURCE D

John Scott was an American volunteer at Magnitogorsk and later wrote the book *Behind the Urals* about his experiences.

It wasn't bad soup. There were some cabbages in it, traces of potatoes and buckwheat, and an occasional bone. It was hot, that was the main thing. The workers ate with relish, some of them having put mustard in it for flavour... The second course consisted of a soup plate filed with potatoes covered in thin gravy, and a small piece of meat on the top.

WORKING CONDITIONS IN THE COUNTRYSIDE

There were few benefits for peasants on the new collective farms. Collectivisation had been achieved by force, and the new kolkhozes were depressing places to be. The peasants were angry about:

- the loss of their own land
- being told what to do by the Collective chairman
- low wages – the income of a peasant working on a collective farm was about 20 per cent of a factory worker's earnings
- long hours and hard physical work – despite the propaganda claims, there were few tractors and machines to help
- lack of freedom – peasants could not leave the collective farms unless they had official permission.

As a result, the peasants worked slowly and put little effort into the tasks. This explains why the collective farms were so inefficient. Instead, peasants put much more their effort into their own, small private plots. Also, despite the dangers of arrest, many ran away to work in towns and cities. Here factory managers, desperate for labour, were often prepared to supply fake internal passports.

ACTIVITY

1 In small groups, draw up a list of the difficulties that workers had to deal with on a daily basis.
2 Repeat this task for peasants.
3 Overall, who do you think had the tougher life: workers or peasants?

EXAM-STYLE QUESTION

A04

SKILLS ANALYSIS, INTERPRETATION, CREATIVITY

Study Extract A. What impression does the author give about the impact of Stalin's collectivisation and industrialisation drive on ordinary people? You must use Extract A to explain your answer.   **(6 marks)**

EXTRACT A

From a book on the Russian Revolution, written by a British historian in 1994.

A society that had scarcely had time to settle down after the upheavals of war, revolution, and civil war a decade earlier was mercilessly shaken up one again in Stalin's Revolution. The decline in living standards and quality of life affected almost all classes of the population, urban and rural. Peasants suffered most, as a result of collectivisation. But life in the towns was made miserable by food rationing, queues, constant shortages of consumer goods including shoes and clothing, acute overcrowding of housing, and endless inconveniences associated with the elimination of private trading.

HINT

To do well in this question, identify the overall message that the interpretation is giving about the impact of Stalin's economic policies on ordinary people. Then use evidence from the interpretation to show how you know this.

4.2 DIFFERING SOCIAL GROUPS, WOMEN AND THE FAMILY

LEARNING OBJECTIVES

- Understand the differences between the main social groups in the Soviet Union
- Understand how family life changed under Stalin
- Understand the extent to which women achieved equality with men in employment and politics.

For an officially classless society, the Soviet Union was far from equal. As has already been seen, living and working conditions varied widely. At the bottom of the pile were the millions of Gulag prisoners. They were used by the Soviet regime as slave labour. Above them were the peasants. For them, life on the collective farms was hard with low wages, long hours and tough physical work. Next came the workers. They too had very poor living and working conditions, although they were paid more than the peasants and had access to slightly better facilities such as factory canteens and town parks. Workers were also divided up, with shock workers and Stakhanovites enjoying far more **privileges** than ordinary workers. Specialists, such as skilled engineers and technicians, were even better paid.

A new class also emerged of Party officials, factory managers and members of the government. These were the ruling class and they were well rewarded for their loyalty to the system. They had access to shops that ordinary citizens could not use. These sold better clothes, food and luxury items. They often lived in special apartment blocks, and in the summer they could even take their holidays at special resorts. However, people in important positions always had the risk of arrest hanging over them if they failed to meet their targets.

WOMEN AND FAMILY LIFE

An old Russian proverb states that 'the harder you beat your wife, the better the soup will taste'. For centuries, Russia had been a difficult place to be female. Women were not considered equal to men. They were not expected to be educated, pursue a career, have strong views or live successful independent lives. Their role was to be an uncomplaining housewife and mother. Domestic violence often by drunk husbands was a common feature of Russian society. When the Communists came to power, they wanted to end this appalling treatment of women. Soon after the revolution, laws were passed to bring about sexual equality. An organisation called the **Zhenotdel** was even established within the Party to promote women's issues.

So did Communist rule really make a positive difference? Stalin argued that it had. In 1930 he closed the Zhenotdel, claiming that its work was done. In 1937, he again felt able to make a major speech declaring how women were now the equal of men (Source E). And indeed, as Source F shows, some women were able to thrive under the Soviet system. For most women, however, this was not the case. While there were certainly some advances, many of the radical ideas first put forward to help women either had no effect against very traditional male attitudes or were steadily reversed by Stalin in the 1930s.

KEY TERM

Zhenotdel the women's section of the Communist Party

SOURCE E

Stalin writing on women's progress in 1937.

The triumph of socialism has filled women with enthusiasm and mobilised the women of our Soviet land to become active in culture, to master machinery, to develop a knowledge of science and to be active in the struggle for higher labour productivity.

SOURCE F

The celebrated female pilots Polina Osipenko, Valentina Grizodubova and Marina Raskova. In 1938, they set a world record for the longest non-stop direct flight by women when they flew nearly 6,000 km from Moscow to the south-eastern tip of Siberia.

ACTIVITY

Study Source F. All three of the pilots were awarded the status of Hero of the Soviet Union, one of its highest awards. Use the worldwide web to research other female Heroes of the Soviet Union. Which story of achievement do you find particularly impressive and why?

CHANGES IN FAMILY LIFE

EXTEND YOUR KNOWLEDGE

In the 1920s, 'postcard' divorces were legal. One partner could end a marriage by sending a postcard to their partner, telling them that the relationship was over.

Many Communists believed that marriage was traditionally a form of **slavery**. The wife became, in effect, the property of her husband and had to submit to his will. When the Bolsheviks seized power in 1917, they set out to change this.

- In order to weaken the authority of the husband, a woman no longer had to take her husband's surname on marriage. She also did not need to gain his permission to take a job.
- To prevent women being trapped in unhappy or abusive relationships, divorce was made easier.
- The Soviet Union became the first European country to legalise **abortion** on demand, in order to give women greater choice over reproduction.
- If couples did marry, it was through a civil rather than a church ceremony. By removing the religious element of the ceremony, the Communists hoped to reduce the status of marriage.

By the 1930s, the unintended consequences of these reforms were beginning to create serious problems for the regime. The Soviet Union went from having the highest marriage rate in Europe to the highest divorce rate. Half of marriages ended in separation. Instead of helping women, the easy availability of divorce was mainly used by men to abandon their wives and children. As a result, many women were left to bring up families entirely unsupported by the father.

The breakup of families also led to gangs of abandoned children living on the streets of towns and cities. They begged, stole and caused trouble. Dealing with this problem took up a considerable amount of government time and resources. Furthermore, the greater use of abortions led to a fall in birth rates. In Moscow in the late 1920s, for example, abortions outnumbered live births by three to one. This was at a time when millions more workers were needed by the state to carry out rapid industrialisation.

A British journalist describing what he saw on his visit to the Soviet Union in the early 1930s.

The orphans were going around in packs, barely articulate and recognisably human, with pinched faces, tangled hair and empty eyes. I saw then in Moscow and Leningrad, clustered under bridges, lurking in railway stations, suddenly emerging like a pack of wild monkeys, and scattering and disappearing.

▶ **Figure 4.2** The 1936 Family Code

Stalin's solution was to call for a return to traditional family values. His message was clear – couples should marry and then stay married. The family came first. As Figure 4.2 shows, a new Family Code of 1936 reversed the radical ideas of the early Bolsheviks. In addition, propaganda was used to criticise men who failed to take their family responsibilities seriously. Stalin's words were quoted frequently: 'A poor husband and father cannot be a good citizen.' One sign of the change in attitude welcomed by many couples was the reappearance of gold wedding rings in shops. During the 1920s, their wearing had been actively discouraged because it was a symbol of the old order. For Stalin, the Family Code was a success. The birth rate rose from 25 births per 1,000 people in 1935 to 31 per 1,000 in 1940, and the divorce rate slowed.

- **The family is the cornerstone of Soviet society.**

- **Unregistered marriages are no longer recognised by the state.**

- **Divorce will be made more expensive.**

- **Men who leave their families will need to support them financially.**

- **Abortion is now illegal.**

- **Being gay is illegal.**

- **Mothers with six or more children will receive money from the state.**

CHANGES IN EMPLOYMENT OF WOMEN

The Communists had always argued that the key to raising the position of women was economic independence. If a woman had a regular income through work, then she would not need to rely on her husband. Work would also develop confidence and self-worth. As a result, the early Bolsheviks were keen to encourage women into the workplace. Soon after the Revolution, laws were passed stating that men and women should be paid the same and be given the same promotion prospects.

During the NEP period, these reforms were slow to have an impact. In 1928, there were just under 3 million women working. This was not particularly impressive for three reasons.

Women factory workers in the 1930s.

'A girl: metro-builder'. Painted by Alexander Nikolayevich Samokhvalov in 1937.

ACTIVITY

Study Sources H, I and J. How did the Communist regime seek to portray women?

- This was similar to the number of women working in Tsarist times, just before the First World War.
- The majority of women were employed in domestic service, farming and small textile workshops, making clothes. These were low-skilled and badly paid jobs.
- Rising unemployment under the NEP led to many women losing their jobs ahead of men.

Stalin's policy of rapid industrialisation transformed the situation. The demand for labour under the Five Year Plans was so high that women became an essential part of the labour force. By 1940, there were 13 million female workers. In addition, women were increasingly working in jobs previously reserved for men. For example, there were female engineers, construction workers, steel makers, train drivers and tractor drivers. By 1940, 41 per cent of workers in heavy industry were women. This represented a huge change from the 1920s.

A sign of the changing times was the promotion of female role models like Pasha Angelina. She organised an all-female tractor team which achieved 129 per cent of its quota, beating all other tractor teams in the region. She was awarded Stakhanovite status, and the state made her a symbol of the new class of highly skilled female workers being created by the Soviet system. Pasha became an official Soviet celebrity. She appeared in propaganda posters and was praised in the media.

Most women's lives were very different from Pasha's. Although they had an increased role, just as in the past, they had to battle prejudice and sometimes anger in the workplace. Some men refused to work with female workers. Despite of the official policy, there was no equal pay – women doing the same job as men were only paid 60–65 per cent of men's wages. Women were also denied opportunities to advance. Most of the highly skilled and management positions were taken by men.

Pasha Angelina (front right) and her tractor team meeting a Soviet politician.

Women also had to cope with the 'double burden'. Despite the demands of full-time work, women were still expected to look after their children and homes. The average man at this time considered these tasks beneath him. The old Russian proverb 'women can do everything; men can do the rest' was still relevant in the Soviet Union in the 1930s. This placed women under great pressure. The state tried to help by offering free childcare until children were old enough to go to school, but not enough places were offered.

CHANGES IN THE POLITICAL POSITION OF WOMEN

KEY TERM

People's Commissar a person in charge of a government department

When the Bolsheviks first seized power, women were given the same political rights as men, including the right to stand for and vote in Communist Party elections. A small group of self-confident, politically committed women rose to important positions. Alexandra Kollontai, for example, became the first female **People's Commissar**. However, this did not mark a new era in female political participation. Despite their public commitment to equality, the Communist Party consistently failed to advance women into politics throughout the period 1924–41. Women like Kollontai remained very much the exception. Many women who did try to rise up in the Party were harassed or ignored. This was because the Party was dominated by men, with old-fashioned attitudes about what women should and should not do. Unsurprisingly, the percentage of women in the Party changed very little throughout the 1920s.

In 1930, the Zhenotdel was closed down, officially because the Communist Party believed that equality had been achieved. This was clearly not true. Instead it reflected the lack of interest that most of the male Party members had in the political role of women. The situation grew worse as Stalin's **Great Retreat** started. In 1936, Stalin approved the creation of the 'Housewives' Movement'. Made up of the wives of Party officials and factory managers, it focused on 'good works' such as collecting money for good causes, organising activities for seriously ill children, and supervising factory canteens and nurseries. The message of this organisation was clear. Politics was for the men. Women should focus on a mothering role. It was not until 1957 that a woman, Ekaterina Furtseva, became a member of the Politburo, the Party's elite decision-making body.

▼ Had women's lives changed for the better by 1941?

▽ NO	▽ YES
■ Traditional sexist attitudes continued.	■ Women played a key role in the economy.
■ Women faced discrimination in the workplace.	■ They carried out jobs previously seen as male.
■ Women were not able to play an important role in politics.	■ The state increased educational opportunities.
■ The Zhenotdel was closed down.	■ Women had equal political rights to men.
■ Women faced the double burden: long hours in the factories followed by all the household tasks.	■ In large factories, women were helped by crèches and laundry facilities.
■ Women were still seen as primarily housewives and mothers.	■ A few women reached high-level positions in government and the economy.

ACTIVITY

In small groups, debate the following **motion**.
'By 1941, the Soviet Union had made significant progress in making men and women equal.'
Take turns arguing both sides of the statement.

EXAM-STYLE QUESTION

A01 **A02**

SKILLS PROBLEM SOLVING, REASONING, DECISION MAKING, ADAPTIVE LEARNING, INNOVATION

'The main effect of Stalin's policies towards women and the family was an increase in female employment.' Do you agree?

You may use the following in your answer:
- female employment
- political participation of women.

You **must** also use information of your own.   **(16 marks)**

HINT

To do very well in this question, you need to explain three factors. That might include the stimulus points, but you must also include a point of your own. For this question, it could be about the increased importance that Stalin placed on marriage and family life.

4.3 CHANGES IN EDUCATION

LEARNING OBJECTIVES

☐ Understand the Communists' views on education

☐ Understand Stalin's reforms

☐ Understand how and why education became more traditional under Stalin.

The Communists took a close interest in the education system because it was seen as the main way to teach the right kind of values to the young. The 1920s saw a lot of experimentation in the way young people were taught, but this was all reversed by Stalin.

EDUCATION POLICY IN 1924

KEY TERM

project method a form of education which involved children being sent into factories to learn skills from the workers, instead of using textbooks in the classroom

By 1924, traditional teaching methods had been largely left behind. Examinations, memorising facts, corporal (physical) punishment and traditional academic subjects were all out. The Communists believed that all these had been used to prepare children for life in a capitalist world, based on values such as competitiveness, rivalry, discipline, patriotism and an acceptance of the Tsarist order. Instead, the Party wanted to prepare children to play a useful role in a communist society. To do this, the '**project method**' was used. This involved sending children into factories where they worked alongside workers. Afterwards they prepared reports on what they had seen and done.

However, schools in 1924 suffered from serious problems, as shown in Figure 4.3. These resulted in a decline in educational standards.

▶ **Figure 4.3** The main problems with education in the 1920s

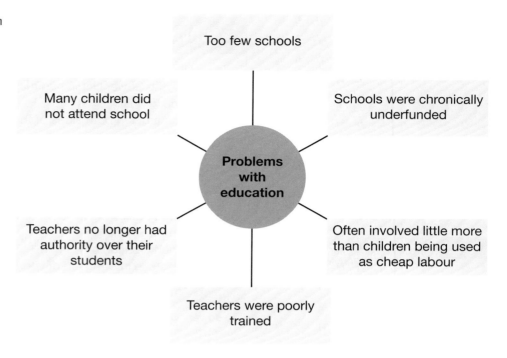

Very few students went to university in 1924, but this did not worry the Communist Party. They regarded universities as elitist institutions, which had served the interests of the rich in the days of the tsar. As a result, universities were allowed to decline. Most traditional **academic** departments were closed down and instead universities taught a few practical subjects to a low level. Many academics, who were regarded as supporters of the old system, were forced out of their jobs. The small number of student places were given to students on a quota basis according to class. The sons and daughters of workers were preferred, with very few places allowed for those with a middle-class background.

SOURCE K

Viktor Shulgin, a Communist with radical views on education. He headed the Institute of Methods of School Work in the 1920s.

You go into the classroom. Everyone stands up. Why do they need to do that?... Why? Well, it is the old residual past; the old dying order: the old type of relationship between adults and children, bosses and subordinates, the teacher and pupil. An awful fart, [a silly or trivial thing] a fart of the past... It must be driven out of the school, driven out.

EDUCATION POLICY UNDER STALIN

Stalin, however, believed that the experimentation of the 1920s had been a disaster. His priority was industrialisation and to make this happen, he needed schools and universities to provide large numbers of disciplined, hardworking and technically skilled students. He also wanted the young to obey the Communist Party without question. As Figure 4.4 shows, in the 1930s Stalin reversed many of the key developments of the 1920s, changing the nature of schooling dramatically.

▶ **Figure 4.4** A typical Soviet classroom in the 1930s

Children had to attend school until at least the age of 15.

To drive up standards, examinations, homework and rote learning of the 'correct' facts became the norm.

The teacher controlled the class with strict discipline.

Students had to sit at desks in rows, facing the teacher with arms folded.

School uniforms came back, including compulsory pigtails for girls.

All schools had to teach reading, writing, the sciences, Russian, geography and history, plus Communist ideology.

Official textbooks were provided by the state and had to be used.

In history, pupils learned about past Russian leaders such as Peter the Great and Ivan the Terrible. These had been dismissed as unimportant in the 1920s.

Fees were introduced for the final 3 years of secondary schooling – Stalin was not prepared to use limited state resources to fund his changes to education.

The changes in schools were reflected in universities. Entry was by competitive entrance exam. There were no longer any limits on the number of middle-class children who could attend. Special emphasis was placed on the study of mathematics, science and technology.

The results were impressive. As the following table shows, the number of young people receiving an education grew markedly over the 1930s. This led to a rise in overall literacy rates, from 55 per cent able to read and write in 1928 to 94 per cent by 1939. The number of students attending university increased from 170,000 in 1927 to 812,000 in 1939.

▼ Improvements in school attendance under Stalin

	1928	1932
The percentage of primary-aged children attending school	60	95

EXTEND YOUR KNOWLEDGE

In the 1920s, Stalin had taken pride in his limited formal education. He told Party audiences that 'he was a crude man'. Reflecting the move back to traditional learning in the 1930s, Stalin started representing himself as a man of culture.

ACTIVITY

Record at least six ways that education differed in the 1930s from what was practised in the 1920s.

EXAM-STYLE QUESTION

A01   **A02**

Explain **two** effects on school children of Stalin's decision to restore traditional values to the Soviet Union's education system.   **(8 marks)**

HINT

To do well in this question, you need to include accurate and relevant historical information to prove your points.

4.4 REASONS FOR, AND FEATURES OF, THE PERSECUTION OF ETHNIC MINORITIES

LEARNING OBJECTIVES

☐ Understand the multi-ethnic composition of the Soviet Union

☐ Understand the treatment of ethnic minorities in the 1920s

☐ Understand how and why Stalin persecuted the Soviet Union's ethnic minorities.

In February 1937, a young Englishman, Fitzroy Maclean, arrived in Moscow to take up a posting at the British Embassy. The future SAS (a specialist British army regiment) hero had a secret ambition: 'I was going, if it was humanely possible, to the Caucasus and Central Asia, to Tashkent, Bokhara and Samarkand.' These were all part of the Soviet Union, but at that time, foreigners were forbidden access to central Asia. Still determined, Maclean boarded a train heading over 1,700 km south from Moscow to Baku on the Caspian Sea. Once there, he illegally boarded a boat which took him further south along the coast to the port of Lenkoran. Staying overnight in the town, Maclean was awoken the following morning by a line of trucks, which continued the entire day, 'driving headlong through the town on the way to the port, each filled with depressed-looking Turko-Tartar peasants under the escort of NKVD frontier troops with fixed bayonets'. Although Maclean did not realise it at the time, these peasants were being deported to central Asia. He had seen the reality of Stalin's extreme and cruel policy towards the Soviet Union's ethnic minorities.

KEY TERM

russification where smaller national groups of the Russian Empire were forced to adopt the Russian language and culture

EARLY SOVIET POLICIES TOWARDS ETHNIC MINORITIES

The Soviet Union was a multi-ethnic nation. A 1926 census by the Communist government listed over 180 different national groups living in the Soviet Union. Working out how to keep this complex country together was an important issue for the Communist Party. The official policy was set down shortly after the October Revolution in the *Declaration of the Rights of the Peoples of Russia*. This promised the different national groups:

- equal treatment
- self-government
- freedom of religion
- the right to develop their own culture and lifestyle.

They could even leave the Soviet Union if they wanted to become independent.

The Communist Party did not want to behave like the Tsarist Empire, in which the smaller national groups were subject to the policy of **russification**. This was also reflected in the unique political structure of the Soviet Union.

- The 15 largest national groups were formed into the Soviet Socialist Republics.
- All the Republics were declared equal, even though Russia was by far the most powerful.
- Minority populations within each Republic were formed into smaller self-governing territories. For example, Russia was divided into 30 national territories.

SOURCE L

The most common nationalities in the Soviet Union, according to the 1926 census, in millions.

▽ TOTAL POPULATION OF THE SOVIET UNION	▽ 147
Russians	77.0
Ukrainians	31.0
Belorussians	4.7
Georgians	1.8
Armenians	1.5
Turks	1.7
Uzbeks	3.9
Turkmen	0.7
Kazakhs	3.9
Kirghiz	0.7
Tatars	0.3

The Communists spoke about the Soviet Union as a 'family of nations'. The different national groups would govern themselves, but together they would form one country. In addition, during the 1920s, each national group was encouraged to celebrate its culture. Schools, books and newspapers used local languages instead of Russian. Local leaders were also trained up and given roles in the Party and government.

ACTIVITY

1 Use the data in Source L to work out the national make-up of the Soviet Union in percentages.
2 On a map of the Soviet Union, record the main locations of the different national groups.

THE TREATMENT OF ETHNIC MINORITIES UNDER STALIN

Within the Party, Stalin was considered an expert on national minorities, mainly because he was Georgian and so from a national minority himself. Lenin had also asked him to develop Party policy on this subject before the revolution. By the 1930s, however, Stalin had no desire to celebrate the Soviet Union's diversity. He was angry at the way non-Russians, such as the Ukrainians, had refused to accept collectivisation. He was afraid that giving too much independence to national groups might weaken overall Communist control. In particular, Stalin was worried that some national groups living near the borders might be disloyal if the Soviet Union was ever invaded.

As a result, Stalin completely reversed the tolerant approach of the 1920s by imposing a new form of russification.
- The celebration of local languages and culture came to be seen as a sign of disloyalty to the Soviet Union.
- As Source M shows, Russian language and culture was shown to be superior to others.
- All schools had to teach Russian as the second language.
- During the purges, many national minority leaders, teachers, artists and writers were arrested.

SOURCE M

Stalin's Victory Day toast to the Russian people in May 1945.

I would like to raise a toast to the health of our Soviet people and, before all, the Russian people. I drink, before all, to the health of the Russian people, because in this war they earned general recognition as the leading force of the Soviet Union among all the nationalities of our country.

KEY TERM

Volga Germans a population of ethnic Germans who lived along mainly along the River Volga in south eastern Russia

Stalin was even prepared to move whole national groups by force if he doubted their loyalty. In 1937, over 171,000 ethnic Koreans were deported from the Soviet Union's Far East to central Asia. Stalin was concerned about the possibility of a Japanese invasion and he thought that the Koreans might support this – he ignored the fact that Japan was violently occupying Korea at the time. In 1941, when the Nazis invaded the Soviet Union, all the **Volga Germans** were arrested and exiled to Siberia and central Asia. As Finland also joined the invasion, 89,000 ethnic Finns were similarly deported.

Stalin's impact on the Soviet Union's ethnic minorities was therefore huge. He ended the tolerant approach of the 1920s and weakened traditional cultures. At its most extreme, whole ways of life were destroyed through forced resettlement. Many national groups developed a long-lasting anger towards the Soviet state as a result.

RECAP

RECALL QUESTIONS

1 How did the 1940 Labour Code punish lateness to work?
2 What was the average size of a family flat in 1940?
3 How did the state try to stop peasants from leaving the collective farms to go in search of better living and working conditions?
4 Name the political organisation that promoted women's rights and was closed down by Stalin in 1931.
5 What women's organisation did Stalin set up in 1936?
6 What happened to divorce and abortion under the 1936 Family Code?
7 Were uniforms, homework, academic lessons and strict discipline a feature of Soviet schools in the 1920s or 1930s?
8 True or false: education levels improved during the 1930s?
9 How many Republics were there in the Soviet Union?
10 Which ethnic group was deported from the Far East of the Soviet Union to Central Asia?

CHECKPOINT

STRENGTHEN
S1 Why were working and living conditions so poor under the Five Year Plans?
S2 Find at least six points that show that the Soviet Union was not an equal society under Stalin.
S3 Find four pieces of evidence that show that ethnic minorities were heavily persecuted under Stalin.

CHALLENGE
C1 Do you think Stalin was right to change the Soviet education system in the 1930s?
C2 Do you think it was better to be a Soviet woman in the 1920s or in the 1930s?
C3 Overall, did life get better for the people of the Soviet Union? To answer this question, go back over the different sections in this chapter, looking for evidence of progress and evidence of things getting worse. Once you have collected all your points, decide where the balance lies.

SUMMARY

- Stalin's policies of rapid industrialisation and collectivisation led to a fall in living and working conditions for workers and peasants.
- In towns, the luckiest workers tended to live in either tiny apartments or barrack style accommodation, while peasants lived in the same poor-quality housing as before.
- During the 1930s, workers and peasants faced increasing restrictions on their everyday lives, including harsh punishments for lateness and internal passports to restrict free movement.
- In the 1930s, society was far from equal. There were clear social groups, separated by different standards of living. Members of the Communist Party, government and factory bosses were part of the privileged elite.
- Under Stalin, women played a much larger role in the economy than ever before, but they still faced discrimination in the workplace and were excluded from significant roles in politics.
- Stalin restored the importance of marriage and family life to the Soviet Union, but this meant women faced the double burden – they had to act as housewives and mothers as well as holding down full-time work.
- Stalin wanted the Soviet Union's education system to produce disciplined and technically trained young people, who could contribute fully to the Five Year Plans. This meant that schools became far more traditional.
- Under Stalin, the early efforts to protect national minorities in the Soviet Union were ended. He believed Russia was the most important nation in the Soviet Union and, out of security concerns, deported whole national groups to Siberia and central Asia.

EXAM GUIDANCE: PART (B) QUESTIONS

A01   **A02**

Question to be answered: Explain **two** effects on the Soviet Union of Stalin's policies towards ethnic minorities.   (8 marks)

> **1**   **Analysis Question 1: What is the question type testing?**
> In this question, you have to demonstrate that you have knowledge and understanding of the key features and characteristics of the period studied. You also have to make judgements about historical events to consider what the effects of them were. In this particular case, it is knowledge and understanding of Stalin's policies towards ethnic minorities and their effect on the Soviet Union.

> **2**   **Analysis Question 2: What do I have to do to answer the question well?**
> Obviously you have to write about Stalin's treatment of ethnic minorities! But it isn't just a case of writing everything you know. You have to write about two effects. Effects are things which the subject you are given causes to happen. The key to explaining the effect of an event is explaining the link between it and an outcome. So, for example, an effect of you doing a lot of revision should be that you can answer the questions in the exam better. You would explain this by emphasising how you know more facts, how you have to spend less time trying to remember things, how you have looked at more examples of how to answer questions, etc.

> **3**   **Analysis Question 3: Are there any techniques I can use to make it very clear that I am doing what is needed to be successful?**
> This is an 8-mark question and you need to make sure you leave enough time to answer the other two questions fully (they are worth 22 marks in total). Remember that you are not writing an essay here. You are providing two effects and enough historical detail to explain why the event had these effects. Therefore, you need to get straight in to writing your answer.
>
> The question asks for effects, so it's a good idea to write two paragraphs and to begin each paragraph with phrases like 'One effect was…' and 'Another effect was…'. The use of phrases in your answer such as 'this led to', 'as a result of this', 'this brought about' and 'this resulted in' will help demonstrate that you are focusing on effects.
>
> The word 'explain' is important because it tells you that you have to do more than just state what the effect was. You need to use your knowledge of the period to explain how the effect led to the outcome. So 'this led to…' states an effect, but 'this led to… because at this time…' is moving towards an explanation.
>
> You cannot get more than 4 marks if you explain only one effect. However, you are required to explain only two effects and you will not gain credit for a third. If you write about more than two, your better two will be credited and the third ignored.

Answer A

Stalin did not treat ethnic minorities very well. This is surprising because he was from Georgia and so from a minority group himself. He had also worked on Communist policy towards ethnic minorities under Lenin and had argued for their equal treatment. From the mid-1930s onwards Stalin followed harsh policies towards ethnic minorities, limiting their rights and freedoms. In total, there were over 170 ethnic groups in the Soviet Union, so Stalin's policies had a big effect on these communities.

The second effect was after the war. Stalin was becoming old, and increasingly bad tempered and paranoid. He was also anti-Semitic. This all combined to make him want to persecute the Soviet Union's Jewish population. Stalin therefore followed a policy which discriminated against this minority group.

What are the strengths and weaknesses of Answer A?
This answer is heading in the right direction. The first paragraph correctly states that from the mid-1930s, ethnic minorities were treated harshly. However, it provides little detail to support this point. Similarly, the decision to focus the second paragraph on the rise of anti-Semitism is a good one, but it needs to include some more examples besides the brief mention of this.

Answer B

One effect of Stalin's policies towards ethnic minorities was a loss of local culture. The Soviet Union was a multi-ethnic state, with over 170 minority groups. When the Communists first took power, they encouraged ethnic minorities to celebrate their own cultures and speak their local languages. The Communists did not want to be seen as cruel like the tsars. However, Stalin did not like local cultures being celebrated. This is because he wanted everyone to have the same outlook and way of life. As a result, in the 1930s all minority groups had to learn Russian as a second language. Many local language newspapers were closed down. The Russian culture was made out to be the best. Celebrating local culture came to be seen as a sign of disloyalty to the Soviet Union and so many people stopped doing it.

Another effect of Stalin's policies towards ethnic minorities was an increase in human suffering. Stalin was paranoid and distrustful and he decided that minority groups living near border areas could not be trusted. These included the Volga Germans and Finns living in the west of the country, as well as Koreans living in the east. He wrongly believed that if the Soviet Union was invaded, these groups would not be loyal. As a result, just before the German invasion of 1941, these minority groups were forcibly relocated by the NKVD to remote areas in central Asia. Being taken away from their homes and forced to start new lives in a harsh landscape was incredibly difficult for those involved.

What are the strengths and weaknesses of Answer B?
This is an excellent answer. It identifies two effects and provides detailed support for them both. There is no need to look for ways to improve this answer, you should just learn from it.

Challenge a friend
Use the Student Book to set a part (b) question for a friend. Then look at the answer. Does it do the following things?

☐ Provide two effects
☐ Provide 3–4 lines of detailed historical knowledge to explain why the event caused the outcome (effect) you have identified.

If it does, you can tell your friend that the answer is very good!

5. THE SECOND WORLD WAR AND AFTER, 1941–53

LEARNING OBJECTIVES

☐ Understand why the Soviet Union was almost defeated by Nazi Germany

☐ Understand the reasons behind the Soviet Union's eventual victory over Germany

☐ Understand what happened Soviet society after the war, as well as the legacy of Stalin's period in power.

The Nazi invasion of the Soviet Union, codenamed Operation Barbarossa, began at 03:15, Berlin time, on 22 June 1941. Three million men, 3,600 tanks and 2,700 planes attacked the totally unprepared Russians. Hitler ordered his forces to flatten the Soviet Union 'like a hailstorm', and warned that 'when Barbarossa commences, the world will hold its breath'. In 1941, the fate of the Soviet Union truly hung in the balance. In his darkest moment, Stalin even said, 'Everything's lost. I give up. Lenin founded our state, and we've screwed it up!' Stalin recovered his nerve, but millions of Soviet citizens died before the Nazi war machine could be halted. Unfortunately for the Soviet people, the long-hoped-for victory did not lead to a better life. Conditions after the war were grim. Increasingly paranoid and terrified of dying, Stalin, the ageing dictator, saw enemies everywhere. He launched a new Five Year Plan to make the Soviet Union the most powerful country on earth, while the threat of the Gulag returned with a renewed series of purges.

5.1 THE SOVIET UNION DURING THE GREAT PATRIOTIC WAR

LEARNING OBJECTIVES

☐ Understand why Nazi Germany almost triumphed over the Soviet Union

☐ Understand why the Soviet Union was able to defeat Nazi Germany

☐ Understand the importance of the Battle of Stalingrad.

THE REASONS FOR AND EXTENT OF SOVIET SETBACKS

Hitler wanted to destroy the Soviet Union. He hated communism, but above all he despised its people. The human race, he wrongly believed, was divided into a hierarchy of races. The German Aryans were the 'master race', while the nationalities of the Soviet Union were categorised as *untermensch* or 'racially inferior'. Hitler wanted to see them beaten and put into slavery. To fulfil his terrible aims, three huge army groups were gathered, supported by troops from Italy, Romania, Hungary and Finland. In June 1941, they began Operation Barbarossa, a three-pronged attack on the Soviet Union. In the first 6 months of the invasion, the Nazis seemed unstoppable, moving forward at a rate of 80 km a day.

- Army Group North advanced through the Baltic States, laying siege to Leningrad by September.
- Army Group Centre advanced due East, taking Minsk by the end of June, then Smolensk. At the end of September Operation Typhoon was launched to capture Moscow. In response, the Soviet government was **evacuated**, and for a short time law and order in the capital collapsed. Shops were looted and people rioted.
- Army Group South advanced through Ukraine, taking the capital Kiev in September, before crossing the River Dnieper and entering Kharkov the following month.

SOURCE A

A German soldier guards Soviet prisoners of war captured during the advance through Ukraine, summer 1941.

Hitler had initially planned on capturing Moscow and Leningrad – the Soviet Union's two major cities – by winter, as he believed that their loss would lead to the collapse of the Soviet state. Although this did not happen, the Soviet Union had been seriously weakened by the end of 1941.

- Over 3 million Red Army soldiers had been captured.
- German forces were in control of 45 per cent of the Soviet population.
- Iron and soviet steel production, both of which were vital for war weapons, had dropped by 60 per cent.
- The country's best agricultural land, which produced around 40 per cent of its grain, was in German hands.

So why had the opening of the war gone so badly wrong for the Soviet Union? One of the main objectives of the Five Year Plans had been to prepare the country for war. Why, despite over 10 years of incredible effort, had the nation not been able to deal with the Nazi attack better? Figure 5.1 gives the reasons for the Soviet Union's initial defeat.

▼ Figure 5.1 The position of the German forces at the end of 1941, and the principal reasons for the Soviet Union's initial defeat

Stalin ignored repeated warnings from his spies and even the British Prime Minister, Winston Churchill, that the Germans were preparing to invade. The Red Army was caught completely by surprise.

Stalin's earlier purge of the Red Army had removed many experienced officers, damaging its fighting ability. Many were hastily released from the Gulags after the invasion.

Stalin forbade his troops from retreating. The fast-moving Germans, however, carried out vast encircling movements. These cut the Soviet forces off, so they were captured.

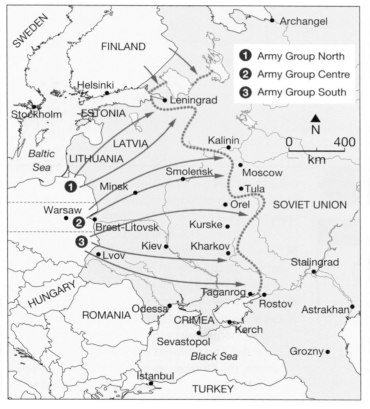

In the first week of the invasion, Stalin retreated to his country house, refusing to speak or give instructions. The Soviet Union was left leaderless.

The German army was formidable. It was huge, highly trained and well equipped. It was also confident after having conquered most of Europe.

The Germans had developed a new military tactic called Blitzkrieg ('lightning war'). This involved using tank forces, massive air power and highly trained troops in co-ordinated, fast-moving assaults. There was little effective defence against this.

ACTIVITY

Compile a list of the major challenges facing Stalin by the end of 1941. Prioritise them in order of importance.

▼ Key events of the Great Patriotic War

YEAR	KEY EVENTS	WINNING SIDE
1941	June: Operation Barbarossa begins. The Soviet air force is almost completely destroyed in the first 3 days of the invasion. September: Operation Typhoon launched to capture Moscow. Leningrad is surrounded by German and Finnish forces and a 900-day siege begins. December: The first Russian counter attack is launched, pushing Germans back from Moscow.	(Nazi flag)
1942	Spring: An early Soviet offensive (attack) fails. June: The Germans launch their summer offensive to capture the oilfields of the Caucasus. July: Germans take Sevastopol. August: German forces begin fighting in Stalingrad.	(Nazi flag)
1943	January: Germans surrender at Stalingrad and the Red Army begins a slow advance. July: The largest tank battle in history takes place at Kursk. The Germans are defeated, losing 2,900 tanks, and 70,000 men are killed. December: By this point, two-thirds of German-occupied territory has been recaptured.	(Soviet hammer and sickle)
1944	January: The siege of Leningrad is ended by a huge Soviet offensive. June: Operation Bagration launched, and 2.4 million Soviet soldiers, 5,200 tanks and 5,300 aircraft advance through Belorussia and into Poland. August: Soviet forces enter Romania and Bulgaria.	(Soviet hammer and sickle)
1945	January: Warsaw, Poland's capital, falls to the Red Army. February: Soviet forces cross into Germany. April: A total of 4,000 Red Army tanks, 23,000 artillery pieces and 4,000 aeroplanes are massed for the assault on Berlin. May: Germany surrenders unconditionally.	(Soviet hammer and sickle)

REASONS FOR THE SURVIVAL OF THE SOVIET UNION

KEY TERMS

counter attack an attack you make against someone who has attacked you

frostbite injury caused by extreme cold

Christmas 1941 was a cheerless time for many people as Europe, from the English Channel to the steppes of Russia, lay under Nazi occupation. There was, however, some hope. Despite the power of Operation Barbarossa, the Soviet state had not collapsed. The following reasons help explain its survival.

■ The start date for Operation Barbarossa was delayed by 5 weeks to allow for the occupation of Yugoslavia. This gave the German army less time to advance into the Soviet Union while weather conditions were ideal.

■ The German advance was slowed and then stopped by winter coming. It began with heavy rain in October, turning roads into rivers of mud. Then in November, snow came and temperatures fell to -35 °C.

■ As Hitler had planned on the Soviet Union collapsing before the onset of winter, the German army had not been properly equipped for cold weather. **Frostbite** became a major issue. German soldiers put newspaper and straw inside their clothing to stay warm. Vehicles and weapons stopped working.

■ In December, General Zhukov launched a Soviet counter attack using tough soldiers from Siberia. Equipped with white snowsuits, goggles, skis, sledges and hardy ponies for moving supplies, they were well prepared for winter fighting. Zhukov's troops also caught the Germans completely by surprise, successfully pushing them back from Moscow.

■ This counter attack was only made possible by accurate intelligence. A Soviet spy based in Tokyo told Stalin that Japan had no plans to attack the Soviet Union in the Far East. This gave Stalin the confidence to transfer large numbers of troops westwards from Siberia.

SOURCE B

A German SS officer describing conditions in the winter of 1941.

Thus we are approaching our final goal, Moscow, step by step. It is icy cold. To start the vehicle engines, they must be warmed by lighting fires under the oil pan. The fuel is partially frozen, the motor oil is thick and we lack anti-freeze. The remaining limited combat strength of the troops diminishes further due to the continuous exposure to the cold. The automatic weapons often fail to operate because the breech locks can no longer move.

- Although the Germans occupied large parts of the Soviet Union, it was far from economically destroyed. The third Five Year Plan had established new industrial areas in the Ural Mountains and Siberia, beyond the reach of German attacks.
- Following the invasion, around 1,500 factories in the west of the Soviet Union were taken apart on Stalin's orders and moved to safety in the east. Some 16.5 million people went with them. Anything of value that couldn't be moved was destroyed in a **scorched earth policy**.
- Stalin helped motivate the nation. He cleverly appealed to people's nationalist spirit by calling on them to defend 'the motherland' and referring to the war as 'the Great Patriotic War'. Little reference was made to saving communism or the Soviet Union. Stalin realised that most people would not give their lives for a political **ideology**.
- In October, Stalin took the decision to stay in Moscow when German forces were approaching. This bold act gave the Soviet people confidence.

KEY TERMS

scorched earth policy the destruction of anything to stop it being taken by the enemy, leaving behind just scorched earth

ideology a set of ideas that refer to a political or social system

ACTIVITY

1 Do you think the Soviet Union survived Operation Barbarossa mainly because of German mistakes, or because of the actions of Stalin and the Soviet people?
2 Discuss this question in small groups, noting down at least three points to support each point of view. Which side has the stronger argument?

THE REASONS FOR THE EVENTUAL SUCCESS OF THE SOVIET UNION

On 24 June 1945, almost 4 years after the start of Operation Barbarossa, Stalin stood at the top of the Lenin mausoleum and watched a great victory parade of the Red Army. The regimental flags of Hitler's armies were symbolically thrown at his feet. Nazi Germany had been defeated. A few months before, on 30 April 1945, Adolf Hitler had committed suicide in his *Führerbunker* while the Battle for Berlin raged above him. On 7 May, Germany had completely surrendered. Stalin and the Soviet people had achieved a remarkable thing. They had driven the might of the German army from the gates of Moscow back to Berlin itself. Figure 5.2 shows some reasons for this.

EXTEND YOUR KNOWLEDGE

Hitler was last seen in public on his 56th birthday on 20 April 1945, awarding medals to the defenders of Berlin. By then he was addicted to a mixture of powerful drugs, including cocaine-laced eye drops. His left arm shook constantly, he suffered from strong stomach cramps and his hearing had been badly damaged following an assassination attempt in 1944. Retreating to his bunker, one of Hitler's last acts was to marry Eva Braun, his mistress of 14 years. During the ceremony on 29 April, Eva wore a black dress and the guests drank champagne. The next day Soviet forces were less than 500 metres from the bunker. At around 3.30 p.m., Hitler shot himself, and his new wife committed suicide by biting down on a cyanide capsule, a fast-acting poison. To prevent his body being taken as a trophy by the Soviets, it was carried outside to a crater, covered with petrol, and burnt.

▶ **Figure 5.2** Reasons for the success of the Soviet Union

The Soviet Union produced more weapons than Germany

The Battle of Stalingrad destroyed Germany's elite Sixth Army

Stalin provided excellent leadership

Reasons for the success of the Soviet Union

Hitler made many bad decisions, which weakened the German army

The Soviet people were tough and would not give in

America supplied weapons, food and transport to the Soviet Union

THE WAR ECONOMY

Germany's failure to defeat the Red Army swiftly in 1941 meant both sides faced a long-drawn-out war. Economic strength became as important as events on the battlefield. Whichever side could produce the most weapons was likely to win the war. In this battle for production, the Soviet Union triumphed. The following table shows that it produced more weapons than Germany.

▼ Soviet and German war production compared

		1941	1942	1943	1944	1945
AIRCRAFT	The Soviet Union	15,735	25,436	34,900	40,300	20,900
	Germany	11,776	15,409	28,807	39,807	7,540
TANKS	The Soviet Union	6,590	24,446	24,089	28,963	15,400
	Germany	5,200	9,300	19,800	27,300	Not known

This impressive economic performance was helped by the following.
- Over half the national income of the Soviet Union was spent on the war. This was a higher proportion than Britain, Germany or America.
- Huge armaments factories were developed in the east of the country, safe from German attack. Chelyabinsk, a city in the Urals, was nicknamed Tankograd because its factories produced most of the famous **T-34 tanks**.
- People worked 7 days a week for the entire length of the war. Factory shifts lasted 12–18 hours.

- Women were used to fill the labour shortage caused by the employment of men into the armed forces.
- The huge Gulag population performed essential war work.

STALIN'S LEADERSHIP

Stalin gave strong leadership throughout the war years. To ensure important military decisions could be taken quickly, he set up and led a Soviet High Command known as STAVKA. This consisted of a small number of leading politicians and generals, plus Stalin, who gave himself the title of Supreme Commander. He also established and led the State Defence Committee (GKO), which ran the economy. This met almost every day of the war. Production problems were identified and measures were taken to try to solve them. Stalin's excellent command of detail made him an able leader of both organisations.

Stalin was also prepared to listen to the advice of others. Following the disasters of 1941, he realised that he did not fully understand how to direct an army. As a result, he promoted able officers and gave them considerable freedom to run the battlefield. General Zhukov stands out in particular. Appointed Deputy Supreme Commander to Stalin in mid-1942, his military achievements included the defence of Moscow, the liberation of Stalingrad and the final attack on Berlin.

SOURCE C

Red Army Commander Georgy Zhukov.

EXTEND YOUR KNOWLEDGE

Following behind the advancing German army were the Einsatzgruppen. These were mobile killing squads, made up of Nazi SS units and German police. They had orders to kill Soviet civilians who were considered to be 'enemies' of Nazi Germany. By the spring of 1943, the Einsatzgruppen had murdered more than a million Jews and tens of thousands of Soviet political officials, Roma (gypsies) and disabled persons. As the German army started retreating, the Einsatzgruppen attempted to remove any evidence of its crimes. Small groups of Jewish labourers were forced to dig up the mass graves and burn the bodies.

THE HEROISM OF THE SOVIET PEOPLE

The Soviet people put up astonishing resistance to the Germans. By the war's end, seven cities had earned the title 'Hero city'. The most famous was Leningrad. In September 1941, its 3 million inhabitants found themselves surrounded by German forces and cut off from the rest of the Soviet Union. This siege lasted 900 days. Hitler, rather than storming the city and causing high German losses, had decided to starve the city into defeat.

The first winter was particularly difficult. Against the background of freezing temperatures and long winter nights of 18 hours, the Germans shelled the city constantly. Water supplies, electricity and heating stopped working. Food rations were cut to near starvation levels. To survive, people ate dogs and cats and made soup from glue and leather. Some of the strongest stole bread from the weakest, while an unknown number ate human bodies. Some 200,000 people died during January and February 1942 alone.

Despite the terrible conditions, the Leningraders refused to give in. The siege was finally broken in January 1944. By then, about 800,000 people had died from shell fire, hunger and cold.

ACTIVITY

By December 1941, the bread ration in Leningrad had been cut to 250 grams a day for workers and soldiers, and 125 grams for everyone else. People survived on around 400 calories per day.
To gain a sense of what these numbers mean, measure them out and compare the results to your own daily food intake.

SOURCE D

A Leningrad doctor recorded a visit to a family in January 1942.

My eyes beheld a horrible sight. A dark room covered with frost, puddles of water on the floor. Lying across some chairs was the corpse of a fourteen year old boy. In a baby carriage was a second corpse, that of a tiny infant. On the bed lay the owner of the room – dead. At her side, rubbing her chest with a towel, stood her eldest daughter. In one day she lost her mother, a son and a brother who perished from hunger and cold.

EXTEND YOUR KNOWLEDGE

On the evening of 9 August 1942, even though the city was surrounded by Germans, a group of starving Leningrad musicians assembled to perform Shostakovich's newly written Seventh Symphony.
The great Soviet composer had dedicated his work to the people of Leningrad. Loudspeakers were hastily set up around the city to broadcast the performance not only to the population, but also to the surrounding German troops. It was an extraordinary act of Soviet defiance.

SOURCE E

A Soviet writer describes visiting his once-beautiful young step sister in April 1942.

Before me now was almost an old woman, withered, with puffy eyelids, darkened face and swollen legs. Her dark, smoothly combed hair was heavily streaked with grey.

ACTIVITY

What can you learn about the Soviet Union during the Great Patriotic War from Sources D and E?

So what motivated the Soviet people to keep resisting? Patriotic duty was important. Many had a natural desire to save their country from foreign invasion. There was a general understanding that Nazi Germany was a uniquely terrible enemy and needed to be defeated. When times were particularly tough, people also turned to religion for comfort. For the length of the war, Stalin ended the persecution of the Orthodox Church and allowed many of its churches to reopen.

The use of force played a role. Punishments for not supporting the war effort were severe. Workers who were 20 minutes late or caught stealing could face imprisonment. As a result of Order 227, soldiers who refused to fight could be put into **penal battalions** and forced to carry out dangerous tasks such as clearing enemy minefields. Alternatively, they were shot. It is estimated that 300,000 Soviet troops were shot by their own commanders.

Certain national groups who were considered potentially disloyal were deported to Siberia and Central Asia, including Volga Germans and Finns. The tiny Soviet Republics of the Caucasus were also targeted. In February 1944, secret police forces entered Chechnya. In an operation lasting just 24 hours, almost all of its population were loaded onto trucks and trains and despatched to Siberia.

SOURCE F

Order 227, issued by Stalin in July 1942.

Not a step back. Each position, each metre of Soviet territory must be stubbornly defended, to the last drop of blood. We must cling to every inch of Soviet soil and defend it to the end.

ALLIED HELP

Following the German invasion, the Americans sent military support to the Soviets under an agreement called 'Lend-Lease'. The Americans ended up supplying the Red Army with:
- 12 per cent of its aeroplanes
- 10 per cent of its tanks
- 2 per cent of its artillery.

American military aid was therefore helpful, but not particularly significant. More important was the American contribution to transport. It kept the Red Army moving, supplying:
- 95 per cent of its trains
- 75 per cent of its jeeps.

Huge quantities of wheat and spam, a type of tinned meat, were also shipped to the Soviet Union. Nikita Khrushchev, the Soviet leader who succeeded Stalin, later wrote, 'Without spam we should not have been able to feed our army.' By 1943, 17 per cent of all calories consumed by the Red Army came from American foodstuffs.

Finally, Britain and America fought against German forces in North Africa, Italy and (after the D-Day landings in Normandy, France in 1944) Western Europe. German cities came under a lengthy attack from British and American bombers. For Stalin, this direct military contribution was too little, too late. As Figure 5.3 shows, for most of the war, he had to face the majority of the German army alone.

▶ **Figure 5.3** German forces on the Eastern Front

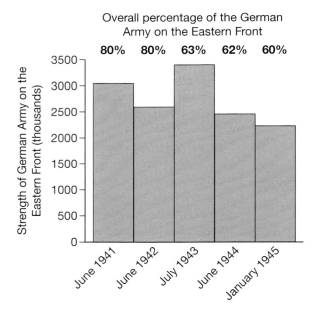

Overall percentage of the German Army on the Eastern Front

GERMAN MISTAKES

The Germans made many mistakes, as Figure 5.4 shows.

▶ **Figure 5.4** A letter Stalin could have written to Hitler!

Dear Adolf Hitler,

Thank you for making the following errors. They helped us greatly.

• Launching your invasion before defeating Britain was a big mistake. It meant you faced a war against two powerful enemies and had to divide your resources.

• You messed up Operation Barbarossa by delaying its start date. You then failed to equip your troops for winter. Everyone knows Russia gets cold!

• You were overambitious. You committed your forces to taking Leningrad, Moscow, Ukraine and the Caucasus. This was reckless and meant your army became overstretched.

• Unlike me, you overruled your generals, even though they often knew better than you.

• Why didn't you let the Sixth Army retreat from Stalingrad when it asked? I was able to capture the lot of them.

• You did not fully turn your economy over to war production. You wanted to maintain people's standards of living. What a joke!

The Soviet People thank you for your help.

Signed,

U. Gaunu

Comrade Stalin

THE BATTLE OF STALINGRAD

One of the key reasons for Soviet victory lay in the Red Army's ferocious defence of Stalingrad, lasting from August 1942 until January 1943. The struggle for this major industrial city on the banks of the River Volga is regarded as one of the Second World War's most important battles. For German soldiers fighting in the ruins of the bombed-out city, it turned into a living nightmare. Captured German diaries show that the Soviets were often referred to as 'devils', mainly because of their determination to fight over every small area of ground. For the defending force, fighting to the bitter end was a question of national survival.

THE REASONS FOR THE BATTLE

Stalingrad was a key objective of the German 1942 summer campaign. The year before, Hitler had promised a quick victory over the Soviet Union, saying, 'You only have to kick in the door and the whole rotten structure will come crashing down.' The failure to win a clear victory meant Germany now faced a long **war of attrition**, and it needed resources in vast quantities, especially oil. As a result, Hitler set his sights on the vast oilfields of Baku in the Caucasus. Their capture would equally deprive the Soviet war machine of its main oil supply, damaging its ability to fight.

In the planned thrust southwards, Stalingrad was identified as a city of strategic importance. As it was at the centre of north–south communication routes, its fall would allow the Germans to stop oil supplies reaching the northern half of the Soviet Union. The fact that it was named after Stalin also made its capture symbolically important for Hitler.

THE COURSE OF THE BATTLE

The German advance south began in June and was initially successfully. By the end of August, the edges of Stalingrad had been reached. Huge air raids then turned much of the city to ruins – opposing the might of the German bombers were mainly young women who volunteered to crew the anti-aircraft guns. Believing the city to be weakened enough, the elite Sixth Army under General Von Paulus started their assault (see Figure 5.5). Their plan was to push through the city to the banks of the Volga River as quickly as possible. The defending Red Army, although outnumbered almost two to one, was determined to prevent this and they fought for every building and street.

Tanks were of little use in the bombed-out city and fighting often became savage hand-to-hand combat. Each side armed themselves with knives and sharpened spades, as well as **sub-machine guns** and hand grenades for close quarter killing. Many of the Red Army counter attacks were launched at night in order to deprive the Germans of sleep and damage their morale. The ruined city also provided ideal territory for **snipers** – the celebrated Soviet sharp shooter Vasily Zaitsev was officially credited with killing 225 enemies in this battle alone.

The Germans referred to Stalingrad as the *kessel* or cauldron, such was the intensity of the fighting. They inflicted an incredible 75 per cent **casualty** rate on the Red Army. One division of 10,000 Soviet soldiers emerged from the battle with only 320 survivors. Despite this, the Red Army troops held their ground, and by November the German advance had stopped.

KEY TERM

war of attrition a strategy involving both sides continually damaging the enemy's personnel, equipment and supplies until one side is defeated

KEY TERMS

sub-machine gun a hand-held lightweight machine gun

sniper a person who shoots from a hidden place, especially accurately and at long range

▶ **Figure 5.5** The German assault on Stalingrad

A German general writing to a friend about the fighting in Stalingrad.

The enemy is invisible. Ambushes out of basement, wall remnants, hidden bunkers and factory ruins produce heavy casualties among our troops.

Part of a letter home written by a German soldier, describing night times in Stalingrad.

If only you could understand what terror is. At the slightest rustle, I pull the trigger and fire off tracer bullets [ammunition that leaves an illuminated trace] in bursts from the machine-gun.

On 19 November, the Soviets made a counter attack, codenamed Operation Uranus. For this, General Zhukov had secretly gathered a force of over 1 million men. He used them to attack the weaker Italian, Romanian and Hungarian troops to the north and south of the city. They were ordered to protect the Sixth Army and their collapse left the Germans alone and surrounded in Stalingrad itself. For the next 2 months, the Sixth Army fought on in increasingly desperate conditions. Despite being forbidden to do so by Hitler, Von Paulus surrendered his army on 31 January 1943.

ACTIVITY

Read Sources G and H. What do they suggest about the strength of morale among the German troops fighting at Stalingrad?

Members of the once-proud German Sixth Army, being led away into Soviet captivity.

THE SIGNIFICANCE OF STALINGRAD

■ For the Soviets, the price of victory was heavy. Half a million soldiers died in the struggle. This was more than Britain lost during the whole of the war. Civilian losses were also high. It is estimated that 40,000 were killed in the first week of the German air-attacks.

■ Most civilians in Stalingrad were evacuated by the Soviet authorities during the course of the battle. After the fighting stopped, they began returning, only to find their city a bombed-out wreck.

■ Some 10,000 civilians, including 1,000 children, were unable to escape and remained trapped in Stalingrad throughout the fighting. They survived by hiding in the cellars of the ruined houses, or down in the sewers. Source J shows the terrible impact this experience had on the young.

■ German losses in Stalingrad were 147,000 dead and 91,000 taken prisoner. Hitler's Sixth Army, which had been the most successful of all Germany's forces since the start of the war, had been destroyed. The forces of Germany's European allies – Hungary, Romania and Italy – were similarly shattered.

■ Stalingrad was Germany's first great defeat, and it proved that Hitler's armies could be beaten. This was a huge psychological boost to the Soviet people. 'You cannot stop an army which has done Stalingrad' became a popular remark. In contrast, the public mood in Germany after Stalingrad was depressed and fearful. So severe was the defeat that the Nazi authorities ordered 3 days of national mourning.

■ Stalingrad was a key turning point in the war. It marked the beginning of the Red Army's slow advance that would finally remove the Germans from the Soviet Union and push them back to Berlin.

■ It boosted the prestige of Stalin and the Soviet Union around the world. Britain celebrated 'Red Army Day' on 22 February 1943. A ceremonial Sword of Stalingrad was made on the orders of King George VI and then presented to Stalin by the Prime Minister, Winston Churchill.

■ Stalin made himself Marshal of the Soviet Union, the military's highest rank. From then on, he always appeared in public in a white military uniform. Zhukov was also promoted to Marshal. To reward the determination of its defenders, Stalingrad was given the title 'Hero City' in 1945.

Written by an American aid worker, who arrived in Stalingrad shortly after the battle to hand out clothing to the civilians.

Most of the children had been living in the ground for four or five winter months. They were swollen with hunger. They cringed in corners, afraid to speak, to even look people in the face.

ACTIVITY

1 Divide into two groups. One group should come up with arguments showing that the Soviet Union's eventual victory over Nazi Germany was mainly because of its own actions. The second group should develop arguments showing that it was mainly because of German mistakes and Allied help.

2 Debate which side has the better arguments.

SOURCE K

Stalin kisses the Sword of Stalingrad. It contained the following inscription in English and Russian.

TO THE STEEL-HEARTED CITIZENS OF STALINGRAD • THE GIFT OF KING GEORGE VI • IN TOKEN OF THE HOMAGE OF THE BRITISH PEOPLE.

EXAM-STYLE QUESTION

A01 **A02**

Explain **two** effects on the Soviet war effort of the Red Army's victory in the Battle of Stalingrad. **(8 marks)**

HINT

To do well in this question, you need to include accurate and relevant historical information to prove your points.

EXTEND YOUR KNOWLEDGE

Of the 91,000 German soldiers taken prisoner, only around 9,000 would ever return to Germany, with the last being released in 1955. The rest died in prison. After Von Paulus was captured, he signed anti-Hitler statements that were broadcast to German troops. He remained in the Soviet Union until 1952, then moved to Dresden in East Germany, where he spent the rest of his days defending his actions at Stalingrad.

SOURCE L

The Soviet newspaper *Red Star* commenting on Stalingrad's significance.

What was destroyed at Stalingrad was the flower of the German Wehrmacht [army]. Hitler was particularly proud of the Sixth Army and its great striking power. It was the first to invade Belgium. It took Paris. It took part in the invasion of Yugoslavia and Greece. In 1942 it broke through from Karkov to Stalingrad. And now it does not exist.

ACTIVITY

Read Source L. Why do you think the morale of the German people was severely damaged by events at Stalingrad?

EXAM-STYLE QUESTION

A01 **A02**

SKILLS PROBLEM SOLVING, REASONING, DECISION MAKING, ADAPTIVE LEARNING, INNOVATION

'The main reason for the Soviet Union's victory over Germany was the strength of its war economy.' How far do you agree? Explain your answer.

You may use the following in your answer:
■ war production
■ mistakes by the Germans.
You **must** also use information of your own. **(16 marks)**

HINT

To do well in this question, make sure you identify at least one additional factor beyond the stimulus points. Ensure you have accurate and relevant historical knowledge to expand on each of your key points.

5.2 THE SOVIET UNION AFTER THE GREAT PATRIOTIC WAR

LEARNING OBJECTIVES

- Understand the efforts taken to rebuild the Soviet economy after the war
- Understand the main groups targeted in Stalin's post-war purges
- Understand popular attitudes to Stalin
- Understand Stalin's legacy to the Soviet Union.

POST-WAR RECOVERY AND THE FOURTH FIVE-YEAR PLAN

▼ The impact of the German invasion on the Soviet Union

Civilian deaths	19 million
Soldiers killed	9 million
Towns destroyed	1200
Villages destroyed	70,000
Railways destroyed	65,000 km
Hospitals destroyed	40,000
Collective farms destroyed	100,000

SOURCE N

A speech by Stalin to Communist officials in the Bolshoi Theatre, February 1946. Also transcribed are the audience reactions.

Our Party intends to organize another powerful upswing of our national economy that will enable us to raise our industry to a level, say, three times as high as that of pre-war industry. We must see to it that our industry shall be able to produce annually up to 50,000,000 tons of pig iron [prolonged applause], up to 60,000,000 tons of steel [prolonged applause], up to 500,000,000 tons of coal [prolonged applause] and up to 60,000,000 tons of oil [prolonged applause]. Only when we succeed in doing that can we be sure that our Motherland will be insured against all contingencies. [Loud applause.] This will need, perhaps, another three five-year plans, if, not more. But it can be done, and we must do it. [Loud applause.]

The Second World War left the Soviet Union economically destroyed. As they left, the German army took anything of value and destroyed the rest. As the table on the following page ('The production of goods in the Soviet Union, 1940–50') and Figure 5.6 show, much of the economic progress achieved in the 1930s was wiped out. By 1945, almost 70 per cent of Soviet industrial production had been lost, while some of the finest showpiece projects, such as the Dnieper Dam, were in ruins. In 1945, Stalin called on the Soviet people to make one last effort. The fourth Five Year Plan was launched to rebuild the country.

A huge 88 per cent of investment went into heavy industry and armaments production. As Source N shows, Stalin saw this as a matter of national security. The rest went into food production and consumer goods – just as in the 1930s, the needs of ordinary people were not considered a priority.

SOURCE M

The heavily damaged Dnieper hydro-electric dam, dynamited initially by the retreating Red Army in 1941 and then again in 1943 by the retreating Germans.

THE PERFORMANCE OF INDUSTRY

The results of the fourth Five Year Plan were impressive. The Soviet economy became the fastest-growing one in the world. Mines, factories and vital road and rail links were all quickly rebuilt. In 1947, the great Dnieper Dam was again producing hydro-electric power. As the following table shows, by the close of the plan, coal, oil and steel production had all gone above pre-war figures, although, as always, statistics from Soviet sources need to be treated with care. As in previous Plans, the production of consumer goods – clothes, shoes and furniture – was a lower priority and failed to reach pre-war levels.

▶ The production of goods in the Soviet Union, 1940–50

		1940	1945	1950
Coal (millions of tonnes)		166	149	261
Oil (millions of tonnes)		31	19	38
Steel (millions of tonnes)		18	12	27
Leather footwear (millions of pairs)		211	63	203

ACTIVITY

1 Use the statistics in the table above to work out the percentage decrease in coal, oil and steel production as a result of the Second World War.
2 Study Source N. 'The applause given to Stalin during his speech shows that his policies were popular.' Explain whether you agree with this statement.

EXTRACT A

An extract from a biography of Stalin, written in 1967.

To many this ambitious programme seemed unreal. The workers to whom Stalin was appealing were hungry – urban consumption had shrunk to about 40 per cent of what it had been in the very lean year of 1940. In the coal-mines of the Donetz Basin men were still pumping water out of the shafts; every ton of coal brought up to the pithead was cherished as a rare treasure. Engineering plants were worked by adolescent semi-skilled labour. People were dressed in rags; many were barefoot. It seemed almost a mockery to urge them to 'catch up' with the United States. Yet the Soviet Union was to attain the major industrial targets Stalin had set; and it was to do so ahead of time.

EXAM-STYLE QUESTION

A04

SKILLS ANALYSIS, INTERPRETATION, CREATIVITY

HINT

Remember not to just copy the extract. You need to say what it makes you think about the Soviet economy.

Study Extract A. What impression does the author give about the Soviet economy in the period after the Great Patriotic War?
You must use Extract A to explain your answer.   **(6 marks)**

The remarkable results owned much to the efforts of the Soviet people. They endured long hours, low pay, food rationing and strict discipline. Extra labour was provided by around 2 million prisoners of war, as well as the huge Gulag population. In addition, a large amount of industrial machinery was taken from Germany. For example, the Opal car factory was taken apart, loaded onto 56 freight cars and put back together in Moscow. By 1947, it was mass-producing the Moskvitch 400 family car, with an impressive acceleration of 0–50 mph in 55 seconds.

SOURCE O

Residents living in the ruins of Stalingrad.

THE PERFORMANCE OF AGRICULTURE

The weakest part of the economy was agriculture. As Figure 5.6 shows, grain harvests had nearly halved over the course of the war. Recovery came only very slowly. Even by 1952, grain production had not regained pre-war levels. This bad result can be explained by a number of factors.

- There was a labour shortage. Many of the men had been killed in the war or moved to the towns, leaving the farming to be carried out mainly by women, children and the elderly.
- There was not enough machinery on the farms due to wartime destruction. Horses, which were capable of pulling ploughs, had also died in large numbers. Women had to pull the ploughs themselves.
- Just as in the 1930s, peasants had little reason to work hard on the farms, as their wages were incredibly low. On Stalin's death, these wages were just one-sixth those of the average factory worker.
- The state put very little investment into improving agriculture. It received a very small amount of the money poured into industry.

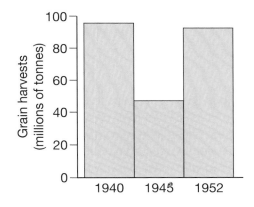

▼ Figure 5.6 Grain harvests

POST-WAR PURGES

Wartime hopes that peace would bring a better life were soon disappointed. Not only did people have to deal with unpleasant living and working conditions, but their leader became increasingly paranoid. Stalin saw threats and plots everywhere, and launched a series of purges to uncover potential enemies. Members of the military, Communist Party, and national minorities were all targeted and the Gulag population almost tripled from 1.6 million in 1942 to 4.7 million in 1947.

EXTEND YOUR KNOWLEDGE

After the war, Stalin's behaviour became increasingly unbalanced, partly reflecting his growing old age. Party leaders lived in constant fear of his unpredictable moods. They would often be invited to long drinking sessions, where Stalin would insult and embarrass them. Later Khrushchev said, 'When Stalin said dance, a wise man danced.'

SOURCE P

A description of Stalin by a prominent leader in the Yugoslav Communist Party.

Stalin was of very small stature and ungainly build. His torso was short and narrow, while his legs and arms were too long. His left arm and shoulders seemed rather stiff. He had quite a large paunch, and his hair was sparse, though his scalp was not completely bald. His face was white, with ruddy cheeks. Later I learned that this colouration, so characteristic of those who sit in offices, was known as the 'Kremlin complexion' in high Soviet circles. His teeth were black and irregular, turned inward. Not even his moustache was thick or firm. Still the head was not a bad one; it had something of the common people, the peasants, the father of a great family about it – with those yellow eyes and a mixture of sternness and mischief.

ACTIVITY

After the war, some people who met Stalin for the first time, having only ever seen his image in propaganda posters, found it hard to recognise him. Why do you think this was?

EXTEND YOUR KNOWLEDGE

Stalin's eldest son, Yakov, an artillery officer, was captured by the Germans in July 1941. Keeping to his view that all prisoners were traitors, Stalin refused German offers to exchange his son for high-ranking German prisoners. Yakov was held in Sachsenhausen concentration camp, and in 1943 he was shot to death by a guard for refusing to return to his barracks.

MILITARY VICTIMS

The 1.5 million Soviet prisoners of war returning from camps in Germany were treated as traitors for allowing themselves to be captured. They were interrogated by the NKVD and most were deported to labour camps in Siberia. The heroes of the war were also victims to Stalin's purges. Marshal Zhukov, the architect of the Soviet Union's victory over Germany, was demoted to command Odessa military district, far from Moscow and lacking any importance. He was also written out of history at that time. The two standard school textbooks on the war, written in 1956, mentioned Zhukov only three times in passing. Other important military leaders suffered similar demotions. In Stalin's mind, these popular and independent-minded leaders were a potential threat to his position. He also did not want anyone else taking the credit for the Soviet Union's victory.

NATIONAL MINORITIES

Terror was used to bring some of the rebellious Soviet republics into line. After the war, nationalists in Ukraine and the Baltic States took up arms and fought to win independence for their countries. These little-known wars were extremely bitter. In Lithuania, for example, Soviet sources admitted to the Red Army losing 20,000 men. Stalin responded with mass deportations. By 1950, this included 300,000 Ukrainians and 400,000 Lithuanians, Latvians and Estonians. The deportations were often carried out in well-planned operations. For example, in Estonia around 3 per cent of the entire population was seized in less than a week in March 1949. Most were women and children.

THE LENINGRAD AFFAIR

Paranoid Stalin believed that officials in the Leningrad Communist Party had become too popular and independent as a result of its heroic role in the war. In 1949, he decided to reinforce his authority by arresting 200 of the Party's leading members. Accused of invented crimes ranging from **corruption** to spying for Britain, these members were sentenced to prison terms of 10–25 years. Around 2,000 more officials were removed from their positions and exiled from their city, losing their homes and other property in the process.

ANTI-SEMITISM

After the war, being seen to have links with the outside world became very dangerous. Stalin regarded 'cosmopolitans', as he called anyone with knowledge of the wider world, as potential spies and traitors. This developed into an attack on the Soviet Union's Jewish population. Stalin had long held

EXTEND YOUR KNOWLEDGE

Molotov was a key figure in Stalin's government, acting as foreign minister from 1939 to 1949. However, he was unable to save his Jewish wife, Polina, from arrest by the NKVD in 1948. Stalin decided that her support for a Jewish homeland within the Soviet Union made her a traitor, and she was sent to the Gulag. Despite this, Molotov continued to serve his master loyally.

anti-Semitic beliefs. He irrationally believed that the Jews of the Soviet Union were not patriotic, and that they had more loyalty to their fellow Jews around the world than to the country. The Jewish community was targeted in the following ways.

- Jews were sacked from positions of responsibility in the government and industry.
- Jewish schools, newspapers and libraries were closed down.
- Jews were thrown out of universities.
- It was made very difficult for Jews to worship freely.
- Leading Jews were imprisoned and sometimes executed.

THE DOCTORS' PLOT

KEY TERM

anti-Semitism prejudice or discrimination against Jewish people

Stalin's **anti-Semitism** grew out of control towards the end of his life. Terrified of dying and increasingly paranoid, he became convinced that those closest to him were trying to kill him. He even had an official food taster to check his meals for poison. When his personal doctor, Professor Vladimir Vinogradov, suggested that Stalin reduce his workload for health reasons, Stalin's suspicious mind turned this into a plot. In 1953, over 30 top doctors, mainly Jews, were arrested on charges of trying to assassinate top Soviet leaders. This number grew to hundreds as the investigation spread. Many historians believe that Stalin was preparing to deport the whole of the Soviet Union's Jewish population to the remote east of the country. However, his death put a stop to this plan, and the arrested doctors were later released.

STALIN'S POPULARITY

Stalin's use of purges, as well as the terrible living and working conditions, does raise the question of how ordinary people viewed their leader. Was he a hated figure, or did he hold a high level of popularity among the Soviet people despite the cruelty of his rule?

As has been seen in Chapter 3, the state certainly worked hard to shape people's opinion of Stalin. They tried to give him an almost god-like status through the cult of personality. This happened even more after 1945 when propaganda depicted him as a military genius, the man who had defeated Hitler. Discovering what the Soviet people really thought of their leader is, however, almost impossible. All the methods commonly used by historians to find out what people thought simply did not exist in Stalin's Soviet Union:

- There were no free elections or alternative political parties to support.
- The press was heavily controlled.
- **Opinion polls** did not exist.
- People were unable to speak freely.

KEY TERM

opinion poll the process of asking a large number of people the same question to find out what most people think about something

Stalin was probably respected and feared in equal measure. Many citizens did feel grateful to him for his wartime role in particular. However, they also saw him as a remote and often terrifying figure. Since no criticism could be published, we are left with praise of him during his rule, but this may have been far from genuine. After his death there was considerable criticism, but that too may have reflected the need of the next leaders to discredit Stalin for political reasons.

THE LEGACY OF STALIN

SOURCE Q

Joseph Stalin lying in state after his death.

KEY TERM

Cold War a war of words and propaganda between the USA and its allies and the Soviet Union and its allies

In the early hours of 1 March 1953, Stalin, aged 73, collapsed in his country house outside Moscow. He had been drinking heavily. Perhaps as a result of Stalin's deep distrust of doctors, or maybe deliberately, his colleagues did not call medical help for at least 24 hours. When a doctor finally arrived and diagnosed a massive stroke, there was little that could be done. Stalin, paralysed, unable to speak, and in considerable pain, slipped in and out of consciousness. He finally died at 9.30 p.m. on 5 March. When the Soviet people were informed the next day, there was a genuine expression of grief. In some of the Gulag camps, however, **revolts** broke out and Red Army units had to be brought in. Later, Stalin was embalmed and put on display with Lenin's body in the renamed Lenin-Stalin Mausoleum. Stalin had been the Soviet Union's unchallenged leader for 24 years.

THE STRENGTH OF THE SOVIET UNION ON THE DEATH OF STALIN

When Stalin became leader in 1929, the Soviet Union was an isolated country, slowly recovering from defeat in the First World War and the ravages of the Civil War. By Stalin's death, it had become an economic and military superpower (see Figure 5.7). Along with the United States, the Soviet Union dominated international affairs. The tension between these two nations plunged the world into the **Cold War**.

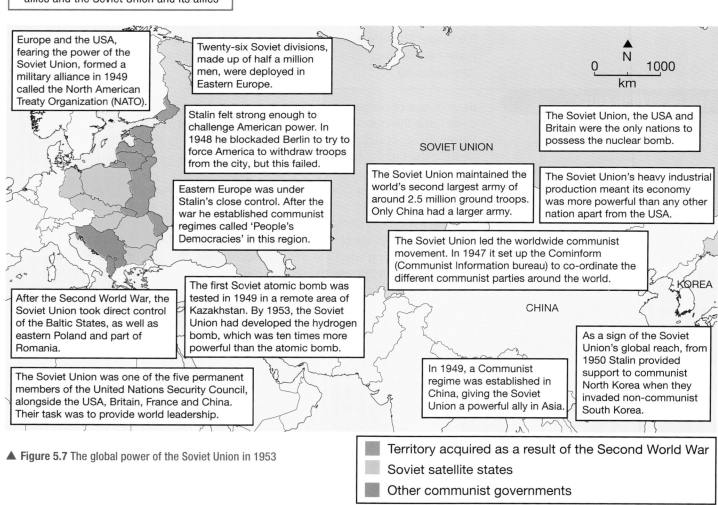

Europe and the USA, fearing the power of the Soviet Union, formed a military alliance in 1949 called the North American Treaty Organization (NATO).

Twenty-six Soviet divisions, made up of half a million men, were deployed in Eastern Europe.

Stalin felt strong enough to challenge American power. In 1948 he blockaded Berlin to try to force America to withdraw troops from the city, but this failed.

Eastern Europe was under Stalin's close control. After the war he established communist regimes called 'People's Democracies' in this region.

After the Second World War, the Soviet Union took direct control of the Baltic States, as well as eastern Poland and part of Romania.

The first Soviet atomic bomb was tested in 1949 in a remote area of Kazakhstan. By 1953, the Soviet Union had developed the hydrogen bomb, which was ten times more powerful than the atomic bomb.

The Soviet Union was one of the five permanent members of the United Nations Security Council, alongside the USA, Britain, France and China. Their task was to provide world leadership.

The Soviet Union, the USA and Britain were the only nations to possess the nuclear bomb.

The Soviet Union maintained the world's second largest army of around 2.5 million ground troops. Only China had a larger army.

The Soviet Union's heavy industrial production meant its economy was more powerful than any other nation apart from the USA.

The Soviet Union led the worldwide communist movement. In 1947 it set up the Cominform (Communist Information bureau) to co-ordinate the different communist parties around the world.

In 1949, a Communist regime was established in China, giving the Soviet Union a powerful ally in Asia.

As a sign of the Soviet Union's global reach, from 1950 Stalin provided support to communist North Korea when they invaded non-communist South Korea.

SOVIET UNION

CHINA

KOREA

0 — 1000 km N

▲ Figure 5.7 The global power of the Soviet Union in 1953

■ Territory acquired as a result of the Second World War
■ Soviet satellite states
■ Other communist governments

THE IMPACT OF STALIN'S PERIOD IN POWER ON THE SOVIET UNION

Stalin's period of rule (see Figure 5.8) had a far-reaching impact on the economic, political and social development of the Soviet Union.

▼ **Figure 5.8** Stalin's period of rule

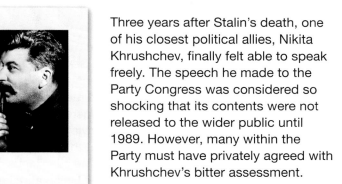

Stalin's period of rule

- A powerful centrally planned economy was created, prioritising heavy industry.
- Consumer industries, used to produce things for ordinary people, were not developed.
- Agriculture was dominated by inefficient collective farms.
- The state made sure that everybody had work.
- Terror was used to control the population, meaning many people lived in fear.
- Millions were imprisoned in the Gulag system for no reason.
- Many people saw Stalin as a god-like figure as a result of a cult of personality.
- Huge power was concentrated in Stalin's hands.
- Traditional values in education, the family and the role of women were revived under Stalin.
- National groups lost their independence, which caused long-lasting resentment.
- Many ordinary people felt they were part of a great project to make their country better.
- All forms of the media were strictly controlled, and independent thought was not encouraged.
- Society was unequal, and party officials and certain groups of workers enjoyed privileges.
- Peasants suffered from extremely poor living and working conditions.
- Individual lives did not matter, and the state allowed millions to die through famine.
- The majority of Soviet citizens viewed their country's role in the Great Patriotic War with great pride.
- The Soviet Union was a world superpower, armed with nuclear weapons and in control of Eastern Europe.

Three years after Stalin's death, one of his closest political allies, Nikita Khrushchev, finally felt able to speak freely. The speech he made to the Party Congress was considered so shocking that its contents were not released to the wider public until 1989. However, many within the Party must have privately agreed with Khrushchev's bitter assessment.

Khrushchev attacked Stalin on many grounds. He read parts of Lenin's Testament, revealing that Lenin had never intended Stalin to be his replacement. He criticised Stalin for the cult of personality and the use of mass terror. He also told the audience that Stalin had failed to prepare the Soviet Union's defences for the German invasion. In 1961, Stalin's body was removed from Lenin's Mausoleum and reburied in a modest grave in front of the Kremlin wall.

SOURCE R

An extract from a speech by the Soviet Union's new leader, Nikita Khrushchev, made to a closed session of the Communist Party Congress in 1956.

It is clear that here Stalin showed in a whole series of cases his intolerance, his brutality, and his abuse of power. Instead of proving his political correctness and mobilizing the masses, he often chose the path of repression and physical annihilation, not only against actual enemies, but also against individuals who had not committed any crimes against the Party and the Soviet Government.

ACTIVITY

There are two distinct views of Stalin's period in power.
1 Stalin was a national hero. He turned an old-fashioned, mainly agricultural country into a modern industrial nation. Although the human cost was high, without this change, the Soviet Union would never have been able to defeat Nazi Germany.
2 Stalin was a cruel monster. He was a cold-blooded killer, who cruelly hurt the people he ruled over. The Soviet Union would have done better without him.
Draw two columns, headed 'National hero' and 'Cruel monster'. Put down as many points as you can think of to support each view.
Once you have collected your evidence, organise a debate with your peers. Overall, do you think Stalin should be remembered as a monster or hero? Take turns arguing both sides.

RECAP

RECALL QUIZ

1   What was the codename for the German invasion of the Soviet Union?
2   How many Soviet soldiers had the Germans captured by the end of 1941?
3   Between 1941 and 1945, did German tank and aircraft production ever overtake that of the Soviet Union?
4   What name was given to the tinned meat supplied by the Americans to the Soviet Union?
5   How many German soldiers surrendered at Stalingrad?
6   What happened to the returning Soviet prisoners of war?
7   What was the main focus of the fourth Five Year Plan?
8   In 1949, which city did Stalin become suspicious of?
9   What type of weapon did the Soviet Union acquire in 1949?
10 What honour was given to Stalin on his death?

CHECKPOINT

STRENGTHEN

S1 Describe the Soviet Union's military position at the end of 1941.
S2 Record four statistics which show the excellent performance of the Soviet Union's wartime economy.
S3 Name two successes and two failures of the Soviet post-war economy.

CHALLENGE

C1 Do you think Stalin should take most of the credit for the Soviet Union's victory in the Great Patriotic War?
C2 Why do you think the Battle of Stalingrad is regarded as one of the key events of the Second World War?
C3 Why did the end of the war not bring an easier life for the Soviet people?

SUMMARY

- In July 1941, Nazi Germany invaded the Soviet Union, achieving initial success. This was helped by Blitzkrieg tactics and Stalin's poor decisions.
- The Soviet Union was eventually victorious because of its war economy, Stalin's ability as leader, the heroism of the Soviet people, help from the Allies and mistakes by the Germans.
- From August 1942 to January 1943, a decisive battle was fought in the city of Stalingrad, leading to the destruction of the elite German Sixth Army. From this point on, the Germans were on the retreat.
- Victory in war did not mean a better life for the Soviet people. Large parts of the Soviet Union had been destroyed, and poor living and working conditions became a feature of life under the fourth Five Year Plan.
- By 1950, heavy industry had largely recovered, although agriculture remained in difficulty. Consumer industries received little investment.
- Stalin became increasingly suspicious after the war, leading to a wave of purges. Returning POWs, elite members of the military, national minorities and communist officials in Leningrad were targeted.
- Making judgements about Stalin's popularity is a difficult task for historians because people were not free to express their views. It is likely that Stalin was both admired and feared.
- When Stalin died in March 1953, the Soviet Union was a world superpower, dominating Eastern Europe and only matched by the United States. Stalin left the Soviet Union with an inflexible political, economic and social system.

EXAM GUIDANCE: PART (C) QUESTIONS

A01 **A02**

SKILLS PROBLEM SOLVING, REASONING, DECISION MAKING, ADAPTIVE LEARNING, INNOVATION

Question to be answered: The main reason for the Soviet Union's victory in the Second World War was the Battle of Stalingrad.
How far do you agree? Explain your answer.

You may use the following in your answer:
- Battle of Stalingrad
- war production.

You **must** also use information of your own. (16 marks)

Analysis Question: What do I have to do to answer the question well?
- You have been given two topics on which to write: the Battle of Stalingrad and war production. You don't have to use the stimulus material provided and can use other factors. However, you will find it hard to assess the role of the Battle of Stalingrad if you don't write about it!
- You must avoid just giving the information. You have to say why the factors you choose helped the Soviet Union win in the Second World War.
- You are also asked to consider whether the Battle of Stalingrad was the **main** reason, so you are going to need to compare reasons.
- You have been given war production as another reason, but you will see that the question says you must use information of your own. So you should include at least one factor other than those you have been given.
- That factor might be Stalin's leadership, the heroism of the Soviet people or German mistakes. If you include one of those, then you have three factors to explain.
- In summary, to score very high marks on this question, you need to give:
  - coverage of content range (at least three factors)
  - coverage of arguments for and against the statement
  - clear reasons (criteria) for an overall judgement, backed by a convincing argument.

Although short, this is a well-focused introduction, which answers the question.

Answer

I partly disagree with this statement because I think war production was a more important reason for the Soviet victory.

This is an analytical paragraph. You advance a range of reasons to explain why the Battle of Stalingrad contributed to the Soviet Union's eventual victory.

Although not the main reason, the Battle of Stalingrad contributed to the Soviet victory. This battle was fought between the German Sixth Army under General Von Paulus and the Soviet army under General Zhukov. It took place from August 1942 to January 1943. It mattered because the German army ended up being defeated. The highly trained and very successful Sixth Amy was destroyed, and 91,000 of its troops were taken prisoners. It was difficult for the German army to recover from such a big defeat. It also stopped Hitler's forces advancing any further south and taking the oil supplies in the Caucasus. This further weakened them as they needed the oil to fuel their tanks. As a result, after Stalingrad the Soviet Army had the upper hand and was able to start advancing.

It is good that you are making sure your first and last sentences clearly connect to the question.

War production was the main reason for the Soviet victory. Stalin knew that the Soviets were only going to defeat Germany if they built more tanks, planes and guns than them. The Soviet Union was able to do this because under the third Five Year Plan a lot of investment went into armaments industries. Furthermore, these were built behind the Ural Mountains, so they were safe from German attack. Also when the war started, 1500 factories were moved eastwards to safety. The Soviets then spent half their annual wealth on weapons. As a result the Red Army was well equipped with large quantities of powerful and reliable weapons like the T-34 tank. This gave it the means to defeat Germany and achieve victory.

Once again, you have written another analytical paragraph. It directly answers the question and you bring good supporting detail.

Stalin's leadership also played a role in the Soviet Union's victory. At the start of the war he actually wasn't a very good leader. He ignored all warnings about the forthcoming German invasion and he did not allow his army to get ready. However, he learned from his mistakes and improved as the war went on. Specifically he did two important things. First, he led the State Defence Committee, which was in charge of the war economy. He was good at this and took decisions quickly, which got problems sorted out. Secondly, he appointed good military commanders like Zhukov and allowed them to take decisions, instead of interfering and spoiling their plans. The economy and army therefore benefited from Stalin's leadership and this contributed to victory.

It is a pity that you were not able to write a brief conclusion on the most important reason.

I therefore partly disagree with the question.

What are the strengths and weaknesses of this answer?

This is a very good answer. It explains three reasons for the Soviet Union's victory in the Second World War. However, there is no attempt to compare the importance of the three factors, which we need for the very highest marks.

Answer checklist
- ☐ Identifies causes
- ☐ Provides detailed information to support the causes
- ☐ Shows how the causes led to the given outcome
- ☐ Provides a factor other than those given in the question
- ☐ Addresses 'main reason' by looking at arguments for and against, and comparing.

GLOSSARY

abortion a medical operation to end a pregnancy so that the baby is not born alive

academic relating to education, especially at college or university level

alliance an arrangement in which two or more countries, groups, etc. agree to work together to try to change or achieve something

armaments industry the business of making of weapons and military equipment

artillery large guns, either on wheels or fixed in one place

assassination the act of murdering an important person

bloc a large group of people or countries with the same political aims, working together

bourgeois following the views of the capitalists

campaign a series of actions intended to achieve a particular result relating to politics or business, or a social improvement

casualty someone who is hurt or killed in an accident or war

civil war a conflict by two opposing sides in the same country

collective (noun) a group of people who work together to run something such as a business or farm, and who share the profits equally

combine harvester an agricultural machine that reaps, threshes, and cleans a cereal crop in one operation

compile to make a book, list, record, etc., using different pieces of information, music, etc.

congress a formal meeting of representatives of different groups, countries, etc., to discuss ideas, make decisions, etc.

constitution a set of rules outlining how a country should be run

corruption dishonest, illegal, or immoral behaviour, especially from someone with power

denunciation a public statement in which you criticise someone or something

discrimination the practice of treating one person or group differently from another in an unfair way

elite people of the highest and usually wealthiest class

empire a group of countries that are all controlled by one ruler or government

ethnic group a community or population made up of people who share a common cultural background or descent

evacuate to send people away from a dangerous place to a safe place

exile a situation in which you are forced, often by political reasons, to leave the area in which you live

expel to officially force someone to leave an organisation

Great Retreat the term used by historians to describe Stalin's rejection of many of the radical cultural and social policies of early Communist rule

impose if someone in authority imposes a rule, punishment, tax, etc., they force people to accept it

industrialise if a country or area industrialises or is industrialised, it develops a lot of industry for the first time

intelligence secret information about the enemy

interrogation the process of asking someone a lot of questions for a long time in order to get information, sometimes using threats

kulak peasant who has become wealthy by using the opportunities provided by the New Economic Policy

left wing a left-wing person or group supports the political aims of groups, such as socialists and communists

legacy something that happens or exists as a result of things that happened at an earlier time

moderate having opinions or beliefs, especially about politics, that are not extreme and that most people consider reasonable

modernisation making something such as a system or building more modern

motion [debate] a proposal that is made formally at a meeting, and then is usually decided on by voting

Ossete a person from a region to the north of Georgia in the Caucasus

overthrow to remove a leader or government from power, especially by force

paralysed unable to move part or all of your body or feel it

persecution cruel or unfair treatment of someone over a period of time, especially because of their religious or political beliefs

plead guilty to state in a court of law that you carried out a crime

private ownership when a company is owned by people or organisations that are not part of the government of a country

privilege a special advantage that is given only to one person or group of people

provisional likely or able to be changed in the future

purge the removal of opponents, often by imprisoning or killing them

quota an official limit on the number or amount of something that is allowed in a particular period

radical radical ideas are very new and different, and are against what most people think or believe

reform a change or changes made to a system or organisation in order to improve it

regime a government, especially one that was not elected fairly or that you disapprove of for some other reason

repressive a repressive government or law controls people in a cruel and severe way

republic a country governed by elected representatives of the people, and led by a president, not a king or queen

resettlement going to live in a new country or area, or helping people do this

revolt strong and often violent action by a lot of people against their ruler or government

revolutionary (person) someone who joins in or supports a political or social revolution

right wing a right-wing person or group supports the ideas and beliefs of capitalism

ruthless so determined to get what you want that you do not care if you have to hurt other people in order to do it

self-sufficient able to provide all the things you need without help from other people

sham someone or something that is not what they are claimed to be

slavery the system of having slaves

spin (politics) to describe a situation or information in a way that is intended to influence the way people think about it – used especially about what politicians or business people do

tank a heavy military vehicle that has a large gun and runs on two metal belts fitted over its wheels

torture an act of deliberately hurting someone in order to force them to tell you something, to punish them, or to be cruel

traitor someone who is not loyal to their country, friends, or beliefs

voluntary done willingly and without being forced

working class the group of people in society who traditionally do physical work and do not have much money or power

INDEX